IDENTIFY YOUR HAPPINESS

DISCOVER AND EMBRACE JOY ALL AROUND

ABHILASH RAJAN

DEDICATION

To my parents, who both, through their actions more than words, taught me the true meaning of the "art of giving." Without their guidance, I wouldn't have reached the point where I even considered having something worth sharing.

FOREWORD

This book stands out for a different reason in a world overflowing with self-help books penned by renowned authors, psychologists, and experts with impressive credentials. "Identify Your Happiness" is written by Abhi—an average person like you and me—who has faced life's trials and tribulations head-on. This book isn't about complex theories or lofty ideals; it's about the real, tangible moments of happiness available to all of us right here and now. Abhi is an incredible individual who has spent years learning the art of finding happiness in the present moment and living consciously, not waiting for some distant future. He has generously shared his wisdom with his family and friends, and now, in these pages, he offers that same wisdom to the world. What makes this book truly remarkable is that it comes from someone who understands the everyday struggles we all face—because he's lived them. "Identify Your Happiness" is a concise read, but do not let its length fool you. Within these pages are powerful insights and actionable steps to help us shift our perspective and find happiness in the here and now. This isn't just another book to read; it's a guide that can transform our lives in ways we might not have thought possible. Whether you are new to the idea of living consciously or someone who's been searching for happiness for years, this book is a must-read. It's short, impactful, and easy to digest, yet it has the potential to make a profound difference in all of our lives. We should approach this book with an open heart and mind. Let Abhi's experiences and insights guide us toward a more fulfilled, joyful life—starting right now.

CONTENTS

PREFACE

Human beings share things and ideas with each other, often to uplift those around them. A wealthy individual might donate resources for a social cause. At the same time, scientists share their expertise to make life easier through innovation. In the same spirit, this book is my attempt to help us all see our life and the world from a fresh perspective by making small but significant changes in our approach to living. After all, clarity is something we all seek.

They say, "The coach appears when the player is ready." But what if there is no coach? Or what if the coach takes longer than expected? In this same regard, we don't need to live by the perception that something or someone will come to change our life. We just need to stop, pause and look around and see that the happiness we seek is already around us. In the meantime, let's get back to basics... shall we?

This book guides you toward finding the clarity that can elevate your life without requiring any drastic changes in your external circumstances. If these shifts in perspective also lead to a more positive environment and influence how others perceive and interact with you, consider that an added bonus.

These are not advices from a spiritual guru, a trained psychologist, or a motivational speaker; rather these are some observations from someone who has experienced life's ups and downs and paid close attention to the details. The truth is, everything we need to know is already right in front of us—the real question is whether we have the eyes to see it.

PROLOGUE

A Personal Anecdote: The Journey Towards Identifying Happiness

As a child, I was the epitome of carefree. I was active, talkative, and, let's be honest, often considered a little bit naughty. My days were filled with laughter, mischief, and an unwavering ability to live fully in the moment. I spent hours making my friends laugh, causing chaos in the most innocent ways, and always feeling like I was at the center of life's adventure. Whether it was sneaking into my neighbor's yard to retrieve a football or planning an elaborate prank for my school friends, I thrived on spontaneity. My parents, no strangers to my antics, would often find themselves shaking their heads in amusement or disbelief as they received yet another call from the neighbors—informing them of my latest misadventure.

Despite the occasional "lesson" in responsibility, I was always able to bounce back with a smile. There was a simplicity to life back then, a lightness in how I processed challenges. Even when I got caught and found myself in trouble, I never stayed upset for long. My mind instinctively found a way to move on. Happiness was never far away at that age and it was always easy to rediscover it.

As I grew older, I poured my energy into sports. I was good at cricket and basketball and by high school, I became the captain of my school's basketball team. Our team wasn't the most skilled; we didn't win often, but we always found a way to make the most of it. The losses never seemed to weigh too heavily on my teammates or me. Instead of dwelling on the scoreboard, we savored the camaraderie, the laughs, and the shared experiences. In those moments, I realized something important—happiness wasn't tied to the outcome of the game, but to the connections we made along the way and just the overall game.

Then came adulthood, with its expectations. Around my late twenties, I married the person I thought was my forever, and we moved to Dubai, eager to begin the next chapter of our lives. We built a beautiful home, had a son, and found ourselves ticking off the boxes of success: a nice car, a steady job, a life that, on the outside, seemed perfect.

But inside, something was missing. I wasn't completely happy in life and was constantly striving for something I couldn't quite define. Despite all the material comforts, I felt a sense of emptiness that I couldn't escape. I thought maybe if I just worked harder, achieved more, or bought a few more things, happiness would eventually appear. But it never did.

The turning point came unexpectedly one afternoon. My ex-wife and I were in India, visiting family. It was a short trip, but it's a moment that I still vividly remember. After some shopping, we found ourselves sitting in the back of a car at a traffic light. Our son was in the back seat with us, and our driver was navigating the chaotic streets of the city. The heat was intense, and the air felt thick with the pulse of a thousand lives rushing by.

As I glanced around, my eyes landed on a group of adults selling small toys at the signal. They moved from car to car, carrying colorful trinkets on trays, their faces glowing with smiles, despite the harsh midday sun. They laughed with each other, joked, and seemed genuinely happy as they went about their work. Their joy, so infectious and raw, made an impression on me that I still carry today.

I couldn't help but wonder: how could they be so joyful with so little? Their happiness was so pure, so free, while I felt disconnected from the joy that my material wealth should have brought. It shook me to my core, and for days afterward, I found myself deep in introspection. I felt a sharp pang of envy.

In the days to follow I often reflected on that moment and would think about my own life and the fact that we had everything my ex wife and I were supposed to want: material success, a beautiful family, a home—yet there was an absence of joy in our lives. I remember asking myself, "How could it be possible that those individuals selling things on the street were so happy with so little, while I had everything I ever thought would make me happy, and yet I felt so… empty?"

That moment—brief and almost unremarkable to anyone else—shifted something deep within me. I realized that happiness doesn't come from what we have or achieve, but from how we choose to engage with life. It's a mindset, a state of being, not a destination.

That realization marked the beginning of a long journey of introspection. I had been chasing happiness like it was something out there to be found, something that could be attained through hard work or the right circumstances. But the truth was, I had been looking in the wrong places. I needed to stop waiting for happiness to come to me and start cultivating it in my everyday life, in the present moment.

Over the years that followed, I began to prioritize myself—my mental and emotional well-being. I started carving out time for activities I loved, things that made my heart light up. I consciously chose gratitude, even in difficult times. I learned that happiness isn't something that arrives as a reward for success, but something that we can choose right now, no matter what life looks like.

This transformation wasn't easy, nor was it linear. There were setbacks, moments of doubt, and frustration. But it was a process worth every ounce of effort. Along the way, I discovered that happiness is less about what happens to us, and more about how we choose to respond. It's about mindfulness, awareness, and being hyper conscious in the moment, even when things aren't perfect.

I share this story with you, not to claim that I have all the answers, but to offer a perspective—one that has helped me find peace and joy in my own life. Happiness doesn't need to be a distant goal. It's not something you'll "get to" one day. It's here, right now, if we open ourselves to it.

I hope that by reading this book, you will also discover that happiness isn't somewhere out there waiting for you to catch up. It's a choice, a practice, and a presence you can cultivate every day.

I hope that my observations & learnings can help you identify happiness in your lives.

CHAPTER 1

LIFE FROM A FRESH PERSPECTIVE

We are all born on a particular date and time - something we have to accept and have no control over. Yet, we spend our lives marking that moment, celebrating it each year as our birthday. Think about it—we never got to choose that date or even our zodiac sign, for that matter, but they become part of who we are. Isn't it interesting how our identity starts to be shaped by things we have no memory of or had any say in? But that's only the beginning.

Fast forward a few years—around 3 or 4—we start collecting memories. We begin identifying the people around us, learning how to communicate with them, and, without realizing it, we also start forming our beliefs. As children, we couldn't wait to grow older. But was it only about being taller or stronger? Not really. We were genuinely drawn to the freedom we saw adults enjoying. So, looking forward—anticipating the future—becomes a natural way of thinking from a young age.

Then comes the teenage years, a whirlwind of energy, new people, ideas, and experiences. Suddenly, we're exposed to different philosophies, situations, and plans. It's a time of rapid change and discovery. We're learning to navigate this new world, figuring out where we fit in. During this stage, we begin mastering the art of survival in society. Some excel and move forward, clear about what they want in life. The rest of us? We often go with the flow, unsure of the next step, yet still moving ahead.

Eventually, we reach adulthood, where we've ticked off many boxes our parents, teachers, and society expected us to. Graduate school? Check. Find a job? Check. But as we went through these milestones, we also constantly shaped our belief system—taking in what the world around us told us was important and often not questioning it.

A belief system that has been taking inputs from all walks of life: religion, nationality, social, and financial status all play a big part in it. Even before we know it, we already carry around with us a personality that not only represents us but also our attitude and approach towards life, while our intelligence continues to knead a perfectly thought-out story around our belief system, assuring us that we are on the right track. This is around the same time that we would go any distance to defend our belief system.

A classic example is our ability to see weirdness or lack of logic in any religious ritual our neighbor follows. Still, we fail to see the same when it happens in our own backyard.

Ever wonder when and how we decide to be biased? The funny part is our intelligence system works in a way that it can detect anything unusual in our surroundings but turns a blind eye when we do something ourselves.

Sooner or later, we all question if there's more to life than chasing after materialistic goals and things. We yearn for real happiness, yet we often feel lost in defining what that means, where to obtain it, and how. We look back on our lives and wonder if our school days were the best and happiest times we ever had. Our minds swiftly conclude, "Yes, those were the days!" But why didn't we realize it when we lived through that time?

As we move on and grow up, our memories flood us with images of good times we had after school—outings with friends, drinks with colleagues, late-night conversations, and those moments of joy that come with promotions and increments. Yet, even then, we fail to recognize the happiness happening right before our eyes.

Why is it that happiness often feels trapped in the past or something we hope for in the future? Why can't it be right here, right now, in our present lives? Why can't we experience it at the moment? Think of a retiree who spends time reflecting on their life, feeling that their happiest moments are behind them. But what if happiness is still present in the peaceful morning walks, the conversations with old friends, or the joy of watching grandchildren play? It's about recognizing that happiness doesn't fade with age— it evolves and can be found in simpler, quieter moments.

Let me explain this further using an analogy of driving your car. Think of the rearview mirror as representing the past—glancing at it helps you understand where you've been, but you can't fixate on it for too long. The windshield, on the other hand, represents the future, what lies ahead. However, the most crucial aspect is the present moment when you're driving the car - the feeling and experience of moving here and now. When you get into the car, you make adjustments to ensure your comfort, adjust the steering wheel, pick your podcast, etc., all to make your drive (present moment) as comfortable and enjoyable as possible. While there are times you need to glance at the rearview mirror, it's essential to stay focused on the road ahead and your surroundings. In the same way, we should acknowledge and learn from our past but immerse ourselves in the present and appreciate what is happening around us. By doing so, we can navigate life more smoothly, enjoying each moment.

We often tell ourselves things like, "I messed up," "I'm in trouble," or "I find this difficult." But when did you last say to yourself, "I'm happy, and I know it"? If that's not something you've done recently, it's time to start. And for those who already do, start counting those moments and note what makes you so happy that you recognize it.

Our body and brain are always listening to us. When we say, "I can't do this," or "I'm not good at something," our body and brain take note, and soon, it becomes our reality. Similarly, when we say, "I'm happy," in a moment of true happiness, our body and brain accept it without contradiction because that moment is proof. That's when our body, brain, and emotions are in sync, and the message is loud and clear: "I'm happy."

Now, imagine using the phrase "I'm happy" every time you feel that way. As you do, you'll find yourself saying it more often. Gradually, you'll realize there are countless happy moments every 24 hours, more than you ever noticed before. This habit gives you a glimpse into the happiness available in the present moment.

But happiness isn't just about recognizing these moments; it's also about creating the capacity to experience them. Happiness comes to us through people, things, situations, thoughts, and experiences. While these can bring joy, not all are under our control. If we depend on them for happiness, we're left at the mercy of chance. But what if we could be the source of our own happiness?

Consider the simple act of making your morning coffee. The aroma of freshly ground beans fills the air, and the warmth of the mug in your hands offers a comforting embrace. Yet, how often do we rush through this experience, our minds racing with the day's tasks? Instead of savoring the moment, we drink coffee while checking emails or planning our to-do list. What if, instead, we paused to enjoy the process, appreciating the rich flavors, the quiet moment of solitude, and the small pleasure it brings to our day? This simple shift in awareness can transform a routine task into a source of happiness.

Imagine coming home after a long day at work to find the kids have done something to make you proud —this moment brings us happiness. Watching your favorite team win a match can lift your spirits. These instances are lovely because they remind us to notice and appreciate the happy moments as they happen.

But what about the days when these external factors do not occur? Accidents don't happen daily, and we can't always rely on outside events to make us happy. So, how do we get the best out of people, things, and situations around us?

The first step is becoming someone capable of receiving more happiness from these external factors. How can we train ourselves to be more receptive to the happy moments that people around us bring?

Consider a scenario where a husband, wife, and children come home happy after their day. The dinner table is filled with laughter, love, and genuine care. What's the secret? Each person showed up for themselves during the day, choosing to see the brighter side of life. Anyone could have had a bad day, but they decided to bring a cheerful mood to the table. What others bring to the table is beyond our control, but what we bring to the table is absolutely under our control.

Happy people create happy environments. A glass of milk spills only milk; in the same way, happiness will spill over into our interactions if we are full of joy. There are no shortcuts to this; we must start spreading what we love to receive.

We must be genuinely involved with those around us to receive more happiness from them. Let's be with them and truly be present when we are together.

Think about the last time you had a conversation with a close friend. Were you fully engaged, listening to their words, and sharing in the moment? Or were you distracted, half-listening while scrolling through your phone, or thinking about what you needed to do next? Imagine the difference if we could be fully present in our interactions, giving our undivided attention to the person in front of us. By truly listening and being present, we strengthen our relationships and find happiness in our shared connection and understanding.

The challenge is that we are not trained to live in the present moment. We're taught to work hard for future rewards from an early age. Studying isn't fun, but good grades are, so we focus on the outcome, not the present. This mindset seeps into other areas of life—doing reps at the gym to reap future benefits of a fit body, enduring long drives to meet a friend without enjoying the drive itself. We don't enjoy the process because our minds are fixated on the future reward.

But what if we could enjoy the process itself? Imagine on a weekend you are driving a car to meet a friend. You have the ability to make the drive as pleasant as possible with all the tools at your fingertips —adjusting the music, setting the perfect temperature, adjusting the seat for comfort—yet we overlook the present moment, rushing to get to our destination, waiting for the real fun to begin. Why did we not enjoy the drive then? Because our minds are fixated on future happiness. We have not been trained to be happy with the present moment; instead, we may talk about the same drive a week later and realize it was wonderful.

Picture yourself at work, completing a task that requires focus and attention. Often, we rush through our tasks, eager to finish so we can move on to the next item on our to-do list. But what if we approached our work with a sense of mindfulness, fully engaging with the task? Whether it's writing a report, solving a problem, or organizing a project, by immersing ourselves in the process, we can find satisfaction and even joy in the act of doing. The sense of accomplishment that comes from a job well done is a form of happiness we might overlook.

Think of a farmer growing fruits. Plucking the fruit is the final stage, but a farmer doesn't postpone happiness until that day. They enjoy the process of nurturing the plants and are involved in every step. We're not surprised by the outcome when we're engaged in the process. We live each moment fully, understanding what we're doing and why, and that makes us better at it and thus happy at the moment.

In addition to these examples, imagine everyday moments: You've just prepared a delicious meal after a long day. The aroma fills the kitchen, and the colors on your plate are vibrant. Still, instead of sitting down to truly enjoy the meal, you find yourself mindlessly rushing through it. Your thoughts are elsewhere—on the emails you must respond to, the chores you haven't yet completed, or the latest news on your phone. Before you know it, your plate is empty, and you barely tasted the food.

Or picture another scene: You're at the beach, and the sun sets, casting a warm golden glow across the sky. The waves gently hit the shore, and there's a peaceful hush as day transitions to night. But instead of soaking in this natural beauty, you're scrolling through social media, looking at pictures of other sunsets, or checking what your friends are up to. The actual sunset, right in front of you, passes by unnoticed.

These are everyday scenarios in which we miss out on the simple joys of life because we're not fully present. The meal that could have been savored, the sunset that could have been a moment of awe and reflection—these moments slip through our fingers because our minds are elsewhere.

What if we took a moment to pause, breathe, and truly engage with the experience? To savor each bite of our meal, appreciating the flavors and the nourishment it provides. Or to put down the phone and watch the sun dip below the horizon, feeling a deep connection to the world around us.

These small shifts in awareness can transform ordinary moments into extraordinary experiences. They remind us that happiness isn't just found in grand achievements or future goals but in simple, everyday moments. By being fully present, we open ourselves to the richness of life, finding joy in the here and now.

It's a win-win situation.

Consider playing your favorite sport and participating in a tournament. If you enjoy each game, not just the final, you'll have memories that last beyond the trophy. Years down the line, people may forget the winner, but you'll still cherish every game if you were genuinely involved in the process.

Don't let the final snapshot with the trophy be the only thing that defines your experience. You're not a sports magazine; you're a human being with the capacity to experience and enjoy much more.

Whether you're a student striving for academic success, a parent working hard for your family, or a retiree reflecting on life's journey, happiness is not the final trophy. It's found in the moments along the way, in the practice, in the laughter, in the small but meaningful experiences that make up our everyday lives.

CHAPTER 2

NATURAL HAPPINESS CALLED NATURE

We all experience moments when we desperately need to disconnect from the stress and chaos that life throws at us. Whether it's a heated argument at home or a stressful meeting at work, there are times when we wish we had a pause button to stop everything, just for a moment. Often, we see people rushing to the smoking area, heading to the coffee machine, or stepping out without a clear destination, all in an effort to escape. Our minds, tirelessly working through every possible solution, eventually become exhausted. Even when we no longer have the energy to engage with these thoughts, our minds refuse to let go, trapping us in a cycle that can last days, weeks, or even longer.

In these moments, we crave a distraction—anything to help us hit that elusive pause button. We turn to movies, call a friend, grab a few drinks, listen to music, or hit the gym. These things may provide short-term relief, but they often leave us longing for something deeper, something that doesn't feel like part of the same cycle we're trying to escape.

Ever noticed how particular we are about our screensavers and desktop images? We choose them carefully because they serve as a form of disconnection from the chaos around us that keeps us consumed 24X7 or a driving force that keeps us sane in this insane world. We might put up a picture of a loved one, a dream destination, or a motivational quote to remind ourselves that our hard work has a purpose—it pays the bills, supports the family, or funds the next holiday. These images help us stay sane in a world that often feels overwhelming, but they also tie us to the things that cause us stress.

But here's a thought—why not try something that's not only free but also infinitely more rewarding? Instead of staring at a screen, step outside and look up. The sky, in all its vastness and ever-changing beauty, is the ultimate live screensaver. It's forcing us to pause and take in the moment. There are no blue light effects, no digital distractions—just pure, natural beauty.

Take a walk in a nearby park or even just around the block. Notice how the breeze feels against our skin, the rustling of leaves in the trees, or how sunlight filters through the branches. These simple, everyday experiences are often overlooked, yet they profoundly affect our well-being. Research has shown that spending time outside reduces stress, lowers blood pressure, and increases our positive mood. Even just a few minutes outside can reset our minds and bodies, providing a sense of calm that's hard to find in our busy lives.

Make it a habit to look at the sky. At first, it might seem like something we've done a thousand times before, but this time, we genuinely observe it. Notice how the clouds form new shapes each day, how the colors shift and blend, creating a new masterpiece every moment. This simple act of observing the sky can transport us to a different world, offering a connection to both nature and yourself. It's a form of meditation, a natural disconnection from the thoughts that otherwise consume us.

Consider the moments when we've felt truly at peace. Perhaps it was during a hike in the mountains, where the sheer scale of the landscape made our everyday worries seem small. Or maybe it was sitting by the ocean, listening to the rhythmic sound of the waves, feeling a deep sense of contentment wash over us. These experiences are not just pleasant memories but powerful reminders of nature's impact on our happiness.

Once we experience this magic and start returning to it regularly, we'll wonder why it took so long to notice. As children, we would lie on the grass, staring at the sky, lost in the wonder of it all. But as we grew up, we lost touch with this simple joy, dismissing it as childish. We've forgotten to enjoy the free gifts that nature has always offered us.

The same goes for oceans, mountains, and rivers. We don't need to engage in any specific activity to enjoy them—

just watching the water flow in a river or the clouds kissing the mountains can be as meditative as anything else. Instead of being lost in thoughts of the past or worries about the future, we can be present, fully immersed in the beauty of nature.

To illustrate, imagine sitting by a river. The water flows steadily, carrying leaves and twigs along its current. As we watch, our mind starts to slow down, mirroring the gentle pace of the water. We begin to notice the small things—the patterns on the stones at the bottom and the way the sunlight sparkles on the surface. Without realizing it, we've stepped out of the stress cycle and into a calm state, all by simply observing nature.

Let's take a moment to appreciate our surroundings, whether we're in the heart of a city or the middle of nowhere. Nature continues its show regardless of whether we pay attention, and it's a show that no human creation can rival. This awareness not only brings us happiness but also keeps us humble. By simply observing and enjoying nature, we can learn more than any book could teach us. A book offers someone else's perspective, but nature provides a personalized experience tailored just for us.

When it comes to teaching silence, nature is the ultimate master. We've all heard the saying, "Empty vessels make the most noise," and it's true—humans often make a lot of noise in an effort to be noticed. But nature, in its quiet wisdom, goes about its business in silence. It's a never-ending process, a constant reminder that sometimes, the most profound things happen in the quiet moments when we stop and listen.

This silence, this stillness—when the noise of our thoughts fades and the world around us calms—is where we find true happiness. In these moments, free from distractions and mental clutter, we connect with a deeper sense of peace and contentment that often eludes us in the busyness of daily life. It's not in the distractions we seek but the quiet moments we frequently overlook. The sound of leaves, the singing of birds, the distant sound of a river—all these are nature's way of reminding us to slow down, to be present, and to find joy in the simple things.

We often search for happiness in big achievements, grand plans, or future aspirations, believing that we must chase or earn joy. But nature teaches us a different lesson. It shows us that happiness isn't out of reach—it's already here, woven into the fabric of our everyday lives. It's like the universe's way of saying, 'Hey, I've been here the whole time; you just had to stop looking for it in your to-do list!'

All it takes is a moment of awareness, a willingness to step outside and let nature in. The next time we find ourselves overwhelmed by the noise of life, remember that the peace we seek is closer than we think. It's in the open sky, the sway of the trees, and the river's flow. Happiness, like nature, is not something to be pursued—it's something to be noticed, embraced, and lived.

So, take a deep breath, step outside, and let nature remind us of the simple truth: happiness is here, all around us, waiting for us to pause, look up, and simply be.

CHAPTER 3

MAGNITUDE OF

NATURE

If we pause and observe the world around us, we begin to see the grandeur of nature in ways that often go unnoticed. Above us, the sun tirelessly journeys across the sky, casting shadows that shift and stretch throughout the day, marking the passage of time. Clouds morph from one whimsical shape to another—one moment a dragon, the next a ship sailing through the blue expanse—reminding us of the constant change in life.

The breeze, whether a gentle caress on a summer afternoon or a brisk gust that carries the scent of rain, is nature's way of communicating with us, urging us to pay attention to the present moment. From the sparrow chirping at dawn to the eagle soaring high above, birds engage in their daily routines, each a tiny yet vital part of the ecosystem, just as we are in the larger tapestry of life.

On the ground, countless species coexist, each playing a role in maintaining the balance of nature. Consider the dandelion, often dismissed as a weed. Yet, it pushes through concrete sidewalks, reminding us of resilience and the beauty in what we overlook. Trees, from the towering redwoods that have stood for centuries to the fragile saplings just beginning their journey, all contribute to the air we breathe, offering life in its purest form. And then there's us—humans—just one species among thousands, all part of the same life cycle. We are born, we grow, we reproduce, and eventually, we return to the earth. It's a humbling thought when you realize that we share this world with many other beings, from the tiniest insect to the largest mammal, each with its own life, purpose, and story.

So, why do we often feel the world revolves around us? How did we come to believe we are more important than a leaf that silently lives and dies? Take a moment to observe a single leaf—notice its intricate veins, how it captures sunlight to create energy, and its transformation from green to vibrant hues in the fall before it gently falls to the ground. This leaf, like us, follows a cycle of life and death. The truth is that we are all part of a grand play directed by nature. In this play, every character—every leaf, every animal, every human—has a role, and we are just one of them. The script is unknown to us, and our time on stage is finite. When a character exits, whether it's a leaf falling, an animal passing, or a human life ending, the play continues. This realization can be unsettling, but it also reminds us of the importance of being present, of appreciating the time we have, just as we might cherish the passing beauty of a sunset or the brief bloom of a flower.

Consider how we cut down a tree, often one that has taken decades to grow, to make room for a road or a backyard. This tree, which once provided shade, shelter for birds, and oxygen for us to breathe, is removed instantly; its life ended for human convenience. In nature's script, there are moments when calamities strike, removing us from the stage just as swiftly—an earthquake that would change the appearance of an entire terrain, floods that take away entire villages, a hurricane that uproots homes, a wildfire that consumes entire forests, or a sudden illness that takes a life. What gives us a sense of superiority over a tree? Is it because we believe we are the chosen ones, adding more value to the world? Yet, if we look closely, we see that the tree's existence was just as vital as ours, contributing to the ecosystem in ways we often fail to recognize. This superiority complex distances us from our true humanity. I'm not suggesting we never cut down trees, but let's acknowledge that trees are as much a part of this universe as we are. By doing so, we stay humble, admitting we are just another character in this vast play.

Gratitude arises when we connect with nature on this level. When we truly grasp our place in the natural world, it becomes easier to surrender our ego. The same ego inflates our sense of self-importance. This ego is particularly persistent if we hold positions of power, influence, or wealth. Imagine a powerful CEO who believes their decisions shape the world, overlooking the janitor who quietly cleans the office at night, ensuring a clean environment for the next day's work. We start to believe that our contributions are more significant than they are, conveniently ignoring those who surpass us—like the teacher who inspired us or the farmer who grows our food—to protect our fragile egos.

Without realizing it, both the CEO and the janitor are replaceable; one day, each will surely be replaced. In other words, no one is truly irreplaceable. The world—and the organization—will continue, with people coming and going in an endless cycle. Yet, in our limited time frame, we tend to believe ourselves indispensable, clinging to a false sense of significance. In truth, our value is not in how much we own or the titles we hold but in the humility we bring to our roles, however big or small.

In our quest for survival, what began as a simple desire to thrive has morphed into a complex game of status and self-importance. We become so engrossed in playing our part that we forget to appreciate the play itself. Picture someone training intensely for a marathon, pushing their body to the limit, obsessed with achieving a personal best. In their single-minded focus, they overlook the beauty of the trail beneath their feet, the melody of birds singing overhead, or the soft crunch of leaves underfoot. Their mind is consumed by the race ahead, convinced that crossing the finish line is the ultimate goal. We miss the beauty of the world around us because we are too absorbed in our pursuits, believing our goals are the most critical aspect of our journey.

To truly enjoy this play of life, we must look around, acknowledge the other actors, and appreciate their roles. Just as a successful theater production relies on the collaboration of writers, stage designers, musicians, and technicians, our lives are enriched by the countless forces at work in nature. Think of a school play—no matter how talented the lead actor, the performance would fall flat without the backstage crew, the lighting, and the supporting cast. No actor, no matter how talented, can shine without the support of others. So, what makes us think our contributions are the greatest? The real magic happens when all elements come together, creating something greater than the sum of its parts.

The food in our refrigerator, neatly stored and ready to sustain us, gives us a sense that we are set for the week ahead. But how often do we pause to appreciate the countless people involved in the process of getting that food to our plate? From cultivation and harvesting to packaging, transporting, and distributing—it's a complex, multi-step process that requires the effort of many hands. Everyone, from the farmer in the field to the truck driver on the road, plays a vital role in ensuring we feel content and cared for. This realization is crucial, as it reminds us that many people are doing jobs we either cannot do or prefer not to do.

Yet, too often, we adopt a mindset of entitlement—thinking, "I earned it, I paid for it, so I deserve it." Of course, money and hard work are essential, but it's equally important to recognize that we are just one small part of a more extensive system. Countless factors must align for everything to come together and function as it does. In this vast web of interdependence, our individual role may seem small. Still, it's part of a much greater process that allows us to enjoy the fruits of others' labor. Gratitude becomes a natural response—not just for what we have, but for the invisible hands that make it all possible.

This sense of interconnectedness is not limited to people and systems—it extends to the natural world around us, where every small detail contributes to a larger, more harmonious whole. When we take a moment to pause and appreciate the beauty of a flower, the vastness of the sky, or the majesty of a mountain, we begin to enjoy the play of life more fully. Imagine standing at the edge of the Grand Canyon, feeling small yet connected to something immense, or watching a bee pollinate a flower, understanding that this simple act sustains entire ecosystems. We become less absorbed in our role and more aware of the production. This shift in perspective enhances our life experience and brings us happiness, humility, and a sense of wonder.

The next time you feel a fresh breeze, take a deep breath—not to improve your health or to outdo anyone else—but to savor the moment. Enjoy the sensation of the air filling your lungs, the connection to something greater. Perhaps it's like standing in the rain, not rushing for cover, but allowing the drops to touch your skin, feeling alive at that moment. That's it. Let's enjoy this nature, this moment, and in doing so, find happiness right here, right now.

As we navigate life, it's easy to become caught up in our roles and goals and pursue what we believe defines our success or worth. But when we step back and recognize that we are just one part of a vast, intricate play directed by nature, we see the world with new eyes. Conscious living is about embracing this awareness—understanding that true happiness is not found in our achievements, status, or roles but in our ability to appreciate the present moment. By observing and connecting with the natural world around us, we learn to live more humbly, gratefully, and joyfully. The real magic lies in the here and now, in the simple act of being fully present and aware, in letting go of our egos and immersing ourselves in the beauty of life as it unfolds. So, as we journey through this grand play, let's remember to pause, breathe deeply, and find happiness in the moment, knowing that this is where life truly happens.

CHAPTER 4

CONTINUOUS STATE OF HAPPINESS IS A MYTH

Just as we are blessed with different senses to experience the world around us, we are also endowed with a wide range of emotions. Our emotional experiences span a range of feelings, including happiness, excitement, anger, sadness, fear, surprise, and disgust, among others. Every external situation may require a different reaction; therefore, it's important to recognize that happiness cannot be a continuous state of mind. We need to understand and accept this fact. This understanding helps us avoid internal conflict when responding to external factors with emotions other than happiness.

Our emotional responses are shaped by what happens around us and what is happening within us. It's not always the good memories from the past that our brain recalls, nor is it always the anticipation of future joys that colors our mood. Sometimes, fear, past regrets, or future anxieties can surface, overshadowing our ability to experience happiness in the present. Think about how often you've been at a family gathering. Still, instead of enjoying the moment, your mind is focused on the upcoming work presentation or a past disagreement with a loved one. In those moments, the laughter and connection around you seem distant because your emotional state is clouded by worry or regret.

Hence, attempting to maintain a state of constant happiness can be exhausting and ultimately counterproductive. The relentless pursuit of happiness without accepting the natural rise and fall of emotions can lead to frustration. It's crucial to understand and appreciate the importance of each emotion without being prejudiced against any of them. Some things trigger us, and some things make us happy. However, the trick is to realize that we respond to various things, and happiness is just one of our reactions. Just as the sun sets to make way for the night, our emotions shift and change, each serving a purpose in our lives. Although happiness is something we all would like to retain as our permanent emotion, if possible.

The key to experiencing ease and fulfillment in life lies in our ability to navigate our emotions fluidly. Just as the ocean's waves rise and fall, emotions ebb and flow through us, each carrying its significance and lesson. Some waves are gentle and bring happiness or joy, while others are more intense, stirring anger or sadness. But each wave, no matter its nature, is an opportunity for growth and understanding. If we are aware or conscious of our present moment, we can identify those waves that bring us happiness. And that can bring a significant change in our lives. Whenever our dearest emotion appears in our lives, it must be enjoyed to the fullest and acknowledged before the next emotion takes over.

Imagine driving in heavy traffic after a long day at work. Frustration builds as every red light and a slow driver tests your patience. In this moment, you may feel anger rising, but by accepting the feeling and allowing it to pass, you avoid letting it ruin the rest of your evening. Just like the traffic clears, your emotions will, too, if you don't cling to them. Imagine a surfer standing on the shore, watching the waves roll in. To ride those waves, he must understand them. As each wave passes, he has a choice: he can resist it, trying to fight against the tide, or he can learn to ride it by syncing with its rhythm and flow. Similarly, we can learn to recognize and understand our own emotional "waves." Over time, we notice patterns—what triggers certain emotions and how they appear in our thoughts and actions. This awareness allows us to consciously engage with our feelings rather than being carried away by them. For example, have you ever noticed how a minor disagreement with a coworker, friend, or partner can leave you feeling irritable for the rest of the day? By identifying the source of that irritation early on, you can choose to address it or let it go, preventing it from affecting your mood or interactions for the rest of the day.

When we embrace our emotions as waves, we stop fearing the stormy seas and start appreciating the ocean. We learn that each wave, whether gentle or fierce, is a part of the vast and dynamic experience of being human. In this way, we can live more fully, accepting every emotion as a vital part of our journey and ultimately finding peace in the flow of life.

Imagine being served a buffet filled with an array of dishes every day at work or college. You walk past this buffet, only to realize you never noticed the dessert section, where the sweetest treats await you. Similarly, we often overlook the small moments of happiness available to us in our daily lives simply because we're too focused on other things.

The more we cultivate awareness of our emotional state, the better we can recognize and cherish these moments of happiness - how lucky we are to witness numerous happy moments each day. One day, you might be running late for an important event or meeting, your mind racing about deadlines, only to have a stranger hold the door open for you with a kind smile. In those small gestures, when you pause to appreciate them, happiness resides—waiting to be acknowledged.

Consider the example of Mark, who wins a luxury cruise for a three-day trip. For someone like him, this is a once-in-a-lifetime experience. As he steps aboard the ship, he enjoys the welcome drink, the snacks, and the lavish amenities in his room. But instead of exploring all that the cruise offers, he focuses only on the things he's familiar with: alcohol, good food, and the swimming pool.

During those three days, he might miss the beauty of the sunrise and sunset from the deck, the luxurious spa, or the entertainment options available to him. Perhaps he even longs for those who aren't with him on this trip. By the time the cruise ends, Mark will have enjoyed some great moments, but if we step back and observe, we realize he missed much of what the journey had to offer. He was so focused on his limited experience—his comfort zone—that he overlooked the vast array of possibilities right before him.

Doesn't this resemble the way many of us live our lives? We often focus on a few select aspects, like family, career, finances, or our social image, while so much more is available to us. We only notice nature when we're on vacation or when it's explicitly pointed out to us. We tend to reserve our attention for a small circle of people, often ignoring the countless others who pass through our lives. We're surrounded by moments of beauty, humor, kindness, and wonder, but many go unnoticed simply because we're not fully present.

Like Mark, who was distracted by the bar menu while others were marveling at a breathtaking sunset from the ship's deck, we, too, are caught up in limited experiences. We may spend hours glued to a screen, only occasionally pausing to notice the world around us. And yet, life—just like a good movie—is a collection of beautiful, meaningful moments, many of which are easily missed if we're not paying attention.

The truth is, we don't need to climb a mountain to experience life in its fullness. Life's richness lies in the small moments—the quiet, meaningful exchanges, the sunsets, the smiles, the acts of kindness. But to truly experience them, we must begin to live more consciously. By embracing the present moment and noticing the beauty in everyday experiences, we can start to appreciate the fullness of life.

Just as Mark had the option to take in everything the cruise offered, we, too, can choose how we experience our lives. It's not about conquering the world or seeking perfection. It's about savoring the moments, acknowledging the joy that exists all around us, and realizing that nothing stops us from thoroughly enjoying life except our perspective.

Our emotions are a natural part of the human experience, offering us insight and growth at every turn. Instead of striving for constant happiness, we can find peace by recognizing and accepting the full range of emotions we encounter. By being mindful of our emotional patterns and the subtle joys around us, we cultivate a more profound, sustainable sense of well-being. Happiness is not about staying in one emotional state but navigating life's waves with awareness and grace. It's time to stop hiding behind excuses.

It's time to let go of the mental prisons we've created for ourselves and start embracing the incredible journey that is unfolding right before our eyes. Don't wait for the trip to be over to realize how much you missed. Start living in the moment, and see how your entire world transforms.

CHAPTER 5

THE RIVER CALLED "LIFE"

Life is like being swept away in a huge river with a group of people, no life jacket, and absolutely nothing to hang on to. Each one of us is on our own. It's a do-or-die situation. What makes it even more frightening is that we have no idea about the depth of this river, the intensity of the waves, or the direction it's headed. Every unknown adds to the desperation. And in desperate situations, people do desperate things. So, naturally, in our struggle to keep our heads above water, we start throwing our hands and legs in all directions. This flailing helps—it keeps us alive.

We realize that as long as we keep moving our limbs, we can survive. The bad news is that it has to be done without break, until our last breath. That's where the real panic kicks in. The process is never-ending, and the chaos that surrounds us is pretty visible. But our visibility is limited—

thanks to the constant splashing all around. With this blurred view, all we see are a few more people who, at first glance, seem to be doing exactly what we're doing. That, strangely enough, gives us comfort. Our brains are wired this way—if others are doing it too, it must be normal. We take it as a sign that we're on the right path, even if it feels like a struggle. We confuse familiarity with truth, and repetition with wisdom. In the absence of clarity, consensus becomes our compass.

But this way of living is exhausting. Keeping our heads above water demands the effort of our entire body. And with that constant effort, fatigue is never too far away. At times, we wonder if the effort is even worth it. Some give up—they stop moving—and almost immediately begin to sink. As soon as they experience the lack of oxygen, something primal kicks in. The part of their brain that thought it wasn't worth the effort takes a back seat. Life itself grabs the wheel. And without thinking, they begin flailing again—refusing to drown. They're back to the surface, gasping, surviving. It becomes clear that survival is instinctive—but awareness is not.

While most continue to struggle, a few people begin to find rhythm in their movements. They discover a certain pattern, a synchronicity in how they move their arms and legs. It's smoother, more intentional, less exhausting. It looks organized. We call it swimming. These swimmers seem to have an advantage. They can stay above water and even steer themselves in desired directions with less effort. Survival becomes more efficient. Life continues. Swimming has become the new norm. And as the saying goes, whatever you practice, you get better at. Soon, we will get better at swimming. Over time, society begins to divide itself:

- expert swimmers—graceful, practiced, admired

- mediocre swimmers—doing okay, still struggling

- non-swimmers—those who haven't figured it out yet

Where we fall within these categories starts to define who we are. It affects how we feel about ourselves—proud, ashamed, driven, or defeated. Our self-worth becomes tied to our swimming skills. Life becomes about improving, competing, comparing. We begin to measure our value not by how alive we feel, but by how efficiently we perform.

Now let's focus on the expert swimmers. From the outside, their lives seem effortless. They navigate the river with skill. They appear confident, composed. They can switch strokes and adjust to new currents. People admire them. But if you ask them—really ask them—many will admit: they're tired. Despite their skill, they're still paddling. Still working. Still putting in constant effort to stay above the water, to stay safe. Even mastery doesn't free them from the need to keep swimming. Behind the grace lies a quiet exhaustion—a silent fear that if they stop, everything might fall apart.

And yet, something unexpected happens to a few of them. One day, amid the flow, they notice a twig passing by gently on the surface. No effort. No struggle. Just presence. Out of curiosity, they wonder: Why can't we glide effortlessly like that twig? They try. At first, nothing happened. They sink. But after some trial and error, something clicks. They stop resisting. They let go. They stop fighting the river. And to their surprise—they float.

For the first time, they move with the river instead of against it. There's no splashing. No panic. They save their energy. And finally, they're able to look around. They see the sky. The greens along the banks. Birds soaring overhead. The sunlight dancing on water. All the things they never noticed while struggling to survive. These moments don't just appear—they reveal themselves when we stop trying to dominate time. Here's the truth: we all have the capacity to float.

But floating requires surrender. Not giving up—but giving in. Letting go of control. Letting go of the obsession with progress, perfection, comparison. The river isn't trying to drown us. It's simply flowing. Floating is awareness. It's the opposite of panic. It's about trusting the river, breathing deeply, and realizing that survival doesn't always mean struggle.

Isn't this how we've been living? What started as a survival mechanism has become our full-time identity. We're so caught up in the race that we forget to ask if the race still matters. We've accumulated more than we can ever consume. More than we can eat, wear, drink, or even breathe in. Survival is already taken care of. Yet we chase—more wealth, more recognition, more security. Constantly.

And so, we forget to look around. We don't stop. We don't question. We never notice that most of what we truly need has been available to us from day one. Peace doesn't arrive with achievement—it arrives with attention. We work our whole lives for success, for fame, for legacy. People want to be remembered even after death. But ask yourself—what's the name of your great-grandmother or great-grandfather? Do you know? Chances are, you don't. That's the shelf life of a human life. And we are no exception.

Let that sink in. Because until it does, we won't take our foot off the gas. It's time to raise our heads, look around, and recognize that all living beings were built to survive—but only humans forgot when to stop. We just kept going. We never asked: is it still necessary?

We can survive with minimal effort—if we stop resisting and start trusting. The swimmer who keeps changing direction does so under the illusion that life will be better over there. But that "better" never arrives. And they never say, "I'm tired," because they worked too hard becoming expert swimmers. How could they admit it wasn't worth it? That would make them look weak. And yet, that's where freedom lies. In honesty. In courage.

The point isn't to abandon survival—it's to realize that it's not the only purpose. Money, career, social image, relationships—these are just dimensions of life and not life itself. So yes, pursue what drives you. But also, learn to float at least on weekends, try spending a few hours where you're not chasing, not proving, not performing. Just be with yourself for yourself.

Notice the design on your bedsheet. The shape of your pillow. The sound of the wind. The plants in your backyard. Let the piece of life that exists in you witness what's always been there. We don't live in a jungle. There's no threat lurking around every corner. There's no force out there trying to drown us. It's all in our heads. The fear of pausing is rooted in the belief that if we stop, we'll fall behind.

Try this experiment: Skip all news for a week. For the first couple of days, you may feel like you're missing out. But when you return, you'll realize—you didn't miss much. The essentials only took 5–10 minutes to catch up on. And yet, how much time do we spend? Consuming news. Debates. Arguments. Analysis. Then discussing all of it—with friends, family, coworkers.

We do it because everyone else does. Birds of a feather flock together. Until we start seeing ourselves as whole individuals / complete units on its own, which may have its own likes / dislikes / preferences, we'll remain trapped in this endless loop. And it's not just news—it's money, too. Look around. So many people are entirely driven by it. Talking about it, thinking about it, chasing it. Every moment. Imagine a friend who only talked about food. Only thought about food. You'd find it strange. But when someone does that with money, we call them smart, ambitious. They become society's expert swimmers.

Let's not forget—these things were created to make our lives easier. They're tools, not masters. Nature has always had a plan. It took care of us before we could speak. We can trust it. There's no need to accumulate endlessly or prove endlessly. Let life unfold. Let go. Float. The moment you float, friction disappears. That's the easiest way to embrace life.

But floating isn't a trick. It's not something you perform—it's something you remember.

Beneath all the effort, all the chasing, all the movement—we already know how to float. We knew it as children, when happiness didn't require achievement and joy wasn't buried under to-do lists or timelines. Somewhere along the way, we traded that natural state for constant striving. Not because we were wrong but because everyone else was doing the same, (splashing water) in the name of survival and no one told us we could stop. Now we know. And knowing makes it a choice.

This isn't about abandoning the swim—it's about realizing you don't need to swim every second to stay alive. You can float. You can rest. You can breathe.

And if that feels unfamiliar now, maybe it's time to return to something more familiar than we remember. Not the goals. Not the titles. But the version of you that felt whole before any of that.

That's where we go next.

It's time to reset.

CHAPTER 6

RESET TO FACTORY MODE

If you're familiar with smartphones' "reset to factory mode" feature, you know it's a way to wipe everything clean—deleting all the apps, settings, and data accumulated over time and returning the phone to its original state. This tool can be valuable for starting fresh or eliminating bugs that slow down our digital devices. But what's the connection of this concept to our lives?

Think back to when we were children. Our default mode was "happy mode". It didn't take much to trigger joy, and it took some external factors to make us unhappy. Even then, those feelings didn't linger. We didn't hold onto grudges, disappointment, or anger for as long as we do now. We would quickly bounce back to happiness, often without even realizing it. As kids, we were natural problem-solvers and lived in the moment.

For instance, when we lose or break a toy, we simply find another one or repurpose something else. A cardboard box became a spaceship, and a blanket transformed into a fort. If the rain stopped us from playing outdoors, we found ways to entertain ourselves indoors, not by dwelling on the weather, but by fully engaging with what was around us. Children don't need elaborate setups or the perfect conditions to be happy—they accept situations as they come. If they can change things, they do. If not, they move on.

However, as we grew up, this ability to move on, to accept things as they are, and to embrace our limitations became harder. We've left our happy version behind. Remember the feeling of contentment when you got your first job? Back then, having a job was enough to make you feel accomplished. Fast forward a few years, and that contentment might have been replaced by stress—stress about promotions, keeping up with expectations, or the pressure to maintain a particular image fueled by the endless comparison game we play, especially with social media.

Wouldn't it be wonderful if we could just reset ourselves to our original "factory mode," where happiness was our default setting? Where we used our intelligence not to complicate life but to simplify it, much like when we were kids. When the size of our house or the brand of our car wasn't necessary, we were content with the basics.

So, what has changed? Why have we become the way we are now? The answer lies in the pressures and expectations that come with adulthood. We've been thrust into a rat race, competing for success, status, and material wealth. As children, a car was just a car. But as adults, our vehicle needs to be better, bigger, and faster than our neighbors. We've become emotionally tied to materialistic things, forming opinions and creating hierarchies in our minds about people and possessions.

This emotional investment in materialistic things runs deep. Whether we realize it or not, we are easily triggered by countless things. News of financial recessions, global conflicts, climate change, or even sports events can stir strong emotions in us. We're constantly bombarded by headlines about Israel and Gaza, Russia and Ukraine, Donald Trump, Vladimir Putin, China, global warming, BBC, CNN, and more. These prove how emotionally invested we are in numerous things, people, and events. For instance, how often has watching a heated political debate or a financial downturn caused you to feel anxious or irritable for hours afterward? Our peace of mind is frequently hijacked by events completely outside our control.

We need to ask ourselves whether we really need to be so invested in these external factors? Is it worth allowing these uncontrollable factors to disrupt our natural happiness?

The challenge, then, is to find a way to reset—to consciously step back from the rat race and disengage from the emotional turbulence it causes. Like children, we need to reconnect with the simple joys of life. This doesn't mean we should ignore our responsibilities or the world. Instead, it's about choosing not to let external factors control our internal state.

We need to accept the world as it is, just as we did when we were young. As kids, we knew our limitations; hence, it was easy to accept situations as they were. Most importantly, we must rediscover that ability to return to our "default mode" of happiness, no matter what life throws at us. After all, happiness isn't something we need to chase—it's already within us, waiting for us to hit the reset button and let it rise to the surface again. By resetting to our "factory mode," we're not turning back time or ignoring the complexities of adulthood. Instead, we're choosing to navigate life with a lighter heart that embraces simplicity, accepts challenges without unnecessary emotional baggage, and finds happiness in the here and now.

The core function of a smartphone is to make and receive calls. Every app we install or every setting we change adds another layer, expanding the phone's capabilities. But over time, some apps drain the battery or take up unnecessary storage, slowing down the phone's performance. That's why we periodically pause to review what's there, uninstalling what we don't need to ensure the phone can perform its most important function without interference or drainage of the battery.

In the same way, it's a good idea, every so often, to pause and check in with ourselves. Where are we spending most of our energy? What's draining us? What activities or relationships are keeping us from performing our core function as human beings—to live in the moment, to experience joy, and to be present? Just like we clear out the clutter on our phones, we need to clear out the clutter in our lives—whether that's emotional baggage, toxic relationships, or negative habits.

Consider this: how do you feel after letting go of a bad habit or a draining friendship? Or after you've adopted a positive habit, like practicing mindfulness or getting regular exercise or learning something new? Often, when we look back, we realize how much lighter we feel. We've freed up emotional and mental space, and as a result, we're able to engage more deeply with life, appreciating the simple things and feeling more grounded and present.

Think about how a small shift in habits can upgrade your experience of life. Maybe you stopped checking your phone the moment you wake up, or you set boundaries in a friendship that was constantly leaving you exhausted. These seemingly small changes can make a huge difference over time, bringing you back to your "factory mode"—where your core function is not bogged down by unnecessary noise.

It's important to regularly reset our internal system, just like we do with our smartphones. When we're mindful of where we're investing our time and energy, we create space for what truly matters—whether that's nurturing relationships, pursuing our passions, or simply being present with what's around us. We become more attuned to what really brings us joy and less distracted by what doesn't serve our happiness.

So, just as a phone needs to be periodically optimized to function at its best, we too need to step back, clear out the unnecessary, and realign ourselves with what brings us back to our true state of happiness. It's not about avoiding the complexities of life but learning how to navigate them with a clearer mind and a lighter heart, letting go of what's slowing us down. By resetting ourselves, we reconnect with our true purpose and begin to live more intentionally, embracing the moments as they come, just as we did when we were kids.

CHAPTER 7

FINDING HAPPINESS SHOULDN'T TAKE MUCH EFFORT

Often, happiness is depicted as a goal, something to chase after or work hard to achieve. We're bombarded with messages that tell us happiness is out there, waiting for us to find it if we try hard enough, or messages about how we can be happier in the future. But what if happiness didn't always require effort or planning? What if, sometimes, it's about simply allowing it to happen—about noticing when it arrives and being open to it without forcing or fabricating it?

Once we realize the importance of acknowledging our happy moments, we often get carried away, trying to recreate or amplify those moments. Think about those moments when happiness sneaks up on us. It could be a spontaneous laugh shared with a friend, the warmth of sunlight on our faces, or the peace we feel sitting quietly. Or it's the unexpected delight during a long commute when, instead of feeling frustrated by a delayed train, we appreciate the cool breeze or use the extra time to catch up on a favorite podcast. Even in mundane tasks, like grocery shopping, happiness can appear in small ways—spotting a favorite snack on sale or running into a familiar face. These moments aren't orchestrated or planned; they happen naturally throughout our day. When we stop trying to control happiness, we often find it right before us, ready to be embraced and felt.

We've all been there—experiencing a joyful moment and immediately wanting to recreate it. Whether it's the thrill of a great conversation, the sound of rain against a window, the feeling of making a perfect shot in basketball, or the simple pleasure of a favorite meal, the temptation to cling to that happiness is strong. But in trying to replicate these moments, we can lose its magic. Instead, if we approach happiness with a light touch—acknowledging it, savoring it, enjoying the moment but not gripping it too tightly—we can give it room to breathe and grow naturally.

Consider the times we've been at a gathering or a party. The best moments often come when we are not trying too hard—simply enjoying the company, music, atmosphere, and food. But when we put too much pressure on ourselves to have fun, it can feel forced, and the moment's enjoyment slips away. The same applies to happiness in everyday life. By easing up on our expectations, we allow it to linger without any force or pressure. Here's an example - imagine dining out with friends. Sometimes, the pressure to pick the perfect restaurant or have an extraordinary experience can overshadow the joy of simply being together. Yet, when plans fall through, and you end up grabbing takeout and sitting in a park, those unexpected, relaxed moments often bring the most happiness—just enjoying good food and company without all the expectations.

As we become more attuned to these moments, we learn to keep ourselves at ease. Happiness doesn't always have to be pursued with intensity; sometimes, it's about creating an environment that allows it to develop naturally. This might mean simplifying our lives, slowing down, or just being conscious without the need to constantly seek more. Imagine spending a weekend without any plans—just letting the day unfold. We might discover the joy of a relaxing breakfast, a spontaneous nap, or walking through our neighborhood. By stripping away the distractions, we notice the happiness that's already present.

We often push it away when we get too desperate to create happiness. Think about a time when you planned a very special day, only to feel disappointed when things didn't go exactly as expected. Trying too hard to force happy moments can make us overlook the simple joys that happen naturally. Happiness tends to show up when we're relaxed and open to feeling it / seeing it, not when we're stressing over making it happen. By letting ourselves be, without always trying to control our emotions/thoughts, we create room for happiness to come to us on its own.

Not all happiness is within our immediate control. Sometimes, we must learn to wait for happy moments to come to us. This doesn't mean being passive or complacent but trusting that life has a rhythm and that happiness will come and go. Think about the moments when you're stuck in extreme traffic. Our first reaction is to be frustrated and stressed, but what if we used that time to listen to music we love, reflect on our day, or observe the world outside our window (trees/flowers/sky)? By shifting our mindset, we can turn a potentially frustrating situation into a peaceful and even happy one. Patience, therefore, becomes a pathway to happiness, allowing us to find joy in moments that might otherwise be overlooked.

Not every situation in life deserves our reaction. Sometimes, the best response is no response at all. This doesn't mean ignoring our emotions or being indifferent, but rather being selective about where we invest our time and energy. Imagine getting caught up in a minor disagreement at work, with a friend at school, or with our roommates. Instead of letting it consume your day, what if you chose not to engage, to let it pass? By not reacting impulsively to every situation, we maintain our inner peace and create room for happiness to grow.

This approach also frees us from the exhausting cycle of emotional highs and lows, enabling a more steady and sustained sense of contentment. The same applies to our online interactions. Have you ever been drawn into a heated debate on social media, only to feel drained afterward? Choosing to disengage in these moments protects your peace and energy, allowing happiness to remain in your control rather than being swayed by others.

This mindset becomes especially important in situations where our first instinct is to react—to defend, to argue, or to 'fix' the moment. But sometimes, the wisest choice is to simply let go and hold onto our inner calm. Real-life situations constantly test this ability. A small annoyance can easily snowball into frustration if we let it. But if we respond with patience and ease, we protect our happiness from slipping away. Let me share a simple but powerful example of this from my friend's recent experience.

My friend Priyanka was on a plane where the lady next to her, Amy, was being quite talkative and obnoxious. Priyanka had been looking forward to a peaceful flight, settling into her window seat with a book. As the flight attendant made their way down the aisle, handing out snacks and drinks, Amy's loud commentary about every little thing grew increasingly bothersome.

When the flight attendant finally reached their row, Priyanka politely asked for a cup of water. Amy, continuing her chatter, took her drink with a careless swipe. In her animated state, she accidentally knocked her drink over, spilling right onto Priyanka's clothes.

Priyanka glanced at Amy, half-expecting an apology. Instead, Amy rolled her eyes and muttered something about "inconsiderate people" under her breath, clearly annoyed by the situation she had caused.

Priyanka could have responded angrily or defended herself at that moment, matching Amy's tone. But she chose to pause and stay silent. Assuming that Priyanka didn't speak

English, Amy continued with more rude remarks, trying to provoke a reaction.

Despite feeling the cold trickle of the spilled drink on her shirt, Priyanka decided not to give Amy's behavior the power to disrupt her peace. She took a deep breath, reached for a napkin to dab at the stain, and then turned her attention back to her book, immersing herself in the story as if nothing had happened.

This experience reminded me that not every situation in life warrants a response. Sometimes, the most powerful action we can take is to choose silence, to rise above pettiness and negativity. By not engaging, Priyanka preserved her own sense of calm and didn't allow Amy's negativity to dictate her emotions.

Priyanka's choice to stay calm in a frustrating moment is a perfect example of how letting go of the need to react can protect our inner peace. She didn't win an argument or prove a point—but she won her own peace of mind. This idea isn't limited to rare, dramatic encounters like hers. In fact, opportunities to practice this mindset show up in the smallest, most ordinary moments of daily life. One such common situation is when we're on the road, dealing with reckless or impatient drivers. These moments, though brief, test our ability to stay composed and not let external chaos dictate our mood.

Another example that many of us have likely experienced is driving and encountering a rash or inexperienced driver. Our immediate instinct might be to overtake them or honk out of frustration. However, if we choose to stay calm and take a breath, we can let the anxiety pass. Chances are that the driver will soon take a turn, speed off, or be on their way without further interaction. These incidents are fleeting moments with a short lifespan, which don't require our reaction or intervention. By remaining calm, we preserve our peace and allow the happiness within us to stay undisturbed. This approach enables us to navigate even the most aggravating situations gracefully, contributing to our overall well-being.

It's easy to get caught up in the heat of the moment and feel that we need to defend ourselves or set the record straight. But often, these reactions only escalate the situation and leave us feeling drained. By choosing silence, we maintain control over our own state of mind, allowing us to focus on what truly matters.

We free ourselves from unnecessary stress when we learn to pick our battles and let go of minor irritations. We also send a message—to ourselves and others—that our peace is not so easily disturbed. This inner strength, this ability to stay composed in the face of provocation, is a key element of lasting happiness.

Patience plays an essential role in this process. It allows us to navigate life's challenges without losing our sense of joy. Patience is not about waiting idly but about maintaining a sense of calm and composure, knowing that good things take time. When we're patient, we're less likely to rush into decisions or actions that might disrupt our peace. In this calmness, happiness often finds its way to us, unexpected but welcome.

Learning to accept things as they are, without constant resistance or the need to change them, transforms us as individuals. This acceptance creates an aura of ease around us, which enhances our well-being and affects those around us. People around us feel more comfortable and relaxed when we're at ease, creating a ripple effect of positivity. Acceptance, therefore, is not surrender but a recognition of life's natural flow, which allows us to go through its ups and downs with joy.

Happiness isn't something we always need to strive for; often, it's about letting go, being patient, and embracing life as it unfolds. By adopting this mindset, we create the space for happiness to naturally emerge, free from the pressure of constant effort or control. The key to happiness often lies in being at ease with the world and, more importantly, ourselves. In this state of ease, we come to realize that happiness is not a final destination to chase, but a continuous journey to experience and enjoy along the way.

CHAPTER 8

WHY DO WE STRUGGLE TO BE IN THE PRESENT MOMENT?

L et's take a closer look at the daily activities that keep us constantly occupied. From the moment we wake up, our first priority is grooming ourselves, ensuring we're presentable for the day. Then comes breakfast—whether we prepare it ourselves or grab something on the go. After that, we dive into our work, which typically occupies most of our day; for less fortunate ones, it could stretch late into the night.

For those fortunate enough to finish work in the evening, there's no shortage of ways to stay occupied: grabbing drinks with friends or colleagues, socializing, dating, hitting the gym, or spending time with family. And if nothing else, there's always the TV, laptop, or smartphone to keep us engaged. Social media alone offers an endless stream of content to scroll through. We can choose from many movies, web series, music, podcasts, or reels if we prefer a quicker fix.

But have we ever noticed how we must rush through even the most basic tasks? We might be in the shower, yet we are already thinking about breakfast. Or, while we are still eating, we are already planning our next move—heading to the office, even though we are not done with our morning routine. We anticipate a fun evening as the workday winds down, yet we're still stuck in the office. And finally when we are out with friends, how often do we find ourselves consumed by our smartphones, scrolling through notifications that we treat as if they're urgent? We waited for this evening the entire day and when that moment appeared we still couldn't be in the present moment.

This begs the million-dollar question: what are we continuously seeking?

The answer is: distraction.

We've become so accustomed to the idea that we must constantly be doing something—anything—that we can't even tolerate a few moments of stillness. Imagine this: you finish your workday and head straight home. Once there, you don't socialize or engage in any "productive" activity. You exist in the quiet of your own company without the need for constant stimulation. Most of us would find this unbearable. Why? Because we're not used to spending time alone with our thoughts. We seek distractions because our minds are rarely content with silence.

From a young age, we form a belief that if we're not actively engaged in a process involving physical or mental activity —we're wasting time. And in a world that values productivity, the idea of "doing nothing" is almost taboo. We see everyone else chasing something: careers, self-improvement, success. If we're not doing the same, we risk being labeled lazy or unambitious.

But have we ever stopped to ask ourselves: Why are we constantly chasing something? Do we really need to pursue all of this so passionately and relentlessly?

This constant chase reinforces our belief that we're heading in the right direction—doing what's necessary to secure a better future. It's like binge-listening to podcasts, convinced each one holds the key to a more fulfilled life. But by the time we've absorbed the information, we're already onto the next episode without ever putting what we've learned into practice. This endless cycle leaves us no time or space to reflect on the value of our consumption. We accumulate information but never allow it to transform into actual knowledge because we don't take the time to apply it. As a result, the information remains just that—information—and eventually fades from our memory. Haven't we all heard someone say, "Oh, I've heard about it somewhere, but I don't recollect it," or "I've read about it but don't remember much." That's the shelf life of information.

Consider our content: celebrity gossip, conspiracy theories, political debates. We spend hours dissecting the latest scandals or controversies—stuff that holds little significance in the grand scheme of things. The truth is that human behavior has followed a predictable pattern throughout history: those in power seek to maintain it, whether through politics, business, war, or media. Yet, we continue to engage with these distractions as if they shape our understanding of the world.

And political content? We all feel well-versed in the ideologies of different parties, cherry-picking information that supports our beliefs. But we fail to realize that politicians aren't here to create a better world—they're the pawns of powerful business interests and master salespeople. These political figures don't answer to the public but to those who fund their campaigns. Meanwhile, we are busy with divisive issues, but we are becoming aware of these via social media. We get occupied in this rat race via scare tactics about financial recession, terrorist attacks, high inflation, and global warming without taking a breather to stop once in a while and ask ourselves where we are heading and why.

It all starts with our notion that we need to keep earning more. Once we have enough for us our immediate excuse to keep chasing more is to secure our kids' future. Ironically, if we are not content with what our parents left us with then what makes us believe that our kids will be content with what we leave for them.

We're all too familiar with the fact that many of us start working and earning right after college, and yet, when we die, we leave vast sums of money in the bank, unused. Why, then, do we keep chasing more? The information we've gathered over time hasn't brought us peace or fulfillment. Yet, we continue to look for the next guru, coach, or "life hack" that promises to make us healthier or happier. The truth is, everything we need to know is already available to us. But instead of facing it—because it requires honesty and courage—we choose the easier path: distraction.

Let's look at a couple of simple examples.

Case 1: If you wake up with a sore throat, you'll go to the doctor, who might ask what you ate the night before. When you mention ice cream, they'll likely recommend you avoid cold foods for a few days, along with some gargles or medicine.

Case 2: If you feel a burning sensation in your chest or stomach, the doctor will likely advise you to avoid spicy or oily foods, eat earlier in the evening, and maybe take some medication.

At its core, most of what we're paying doctors for is common sense. We know we shouldn't indulge in certain behaviors, but we give in to temptation anyway. I'm not downplaying the importance of doctors. Still, our intelligence often goes out the window when we're seeking temporary pleasure. All it takes is a good commercial or peer pressure or our self-declared cheat day to ignite the urge for that ice cream/alcohol/cigarettes / oily-spicy junk food. Our bodies respond to everything we consume but we are too occupied to notice that. It's all too easy to ignore our body's signals until the discomfort becomes unbearable.

Take back pain, for instance. Most doctors will tell you to avoid lifting heavy objects incorrectly—essential advice we could figure out on our own common sense if we were actually paying attention to our bodies. But we outsource everything to experts, forgetting that no one can track our movements and sensations better than we can.

We wait for things to get terrible before we take action, relying on medical leave to cope with ongoing discomfort. We avoid taking full responsibility for our health, yet we have no problem indulging in harmful behaviors. Suppose you were tricked into drinking alcohol disguised as juice. In that case, you'd still feel tipsy—because your body responds to what you consume, regardless of your awareness. The first signals are always there, but we're too distracted to notice.

Living a life of constant distraction is one of the main contributors to poor health—both physical and mental. The information we absorb—whether consciously or unconsciously—shapes our beliefs and actions. We rarely stop to consider the source or validity of the beliefs we're forming because we're too busy seeking the next distraction.

Here's the scary truth: "if you don't take charge of your life, someone else will". You don't need to advertise your availability; they'll find you. They'll mold you, control your thinking, and dictate your actions. And you'll believe it's all your choice.

CHAPTER 9

SELF CARE – LOVE YOURSELF FIRST

Before we can even begin to talk about self-care, we must first ask—who are we, really? Beneath the roles, labels, and expectations placed on us by society, who is the person we're actually trying to take care of?

Let's take a hypothetical example for a moment. Imagine you were the only living person on this earth and had never seen another human being. In this situation, how would you perceive yourself? Would you consider yourself tall or short? Dark or fair? Rich or poor? Optimist or pessimist? A man or a woman? Young or old? Quick-tempered or patient? Believer or non-believer? Workaholic or lazy? Over ambitious or realistic? And the list goes on.

Do you see how many of these labels exist only because we live in a society that hands them to us? Whether we feel good or bad about these tags, we rarely stop to question how many of them we've accepted as part of who we are. Our entire self-image becomes entangled in these comparisons, most of which have little to do with who we truly are.

Now, for just a minute, imagine peeling away everything that society made you put on. What remains is you. Just you. That realization alone can change your life. And once you see it, you might find yourself wanting to spend more and more time with that version of yourself—the real you, stripped of outside expectations and labels.

We often say that every individual is different, but how deeply do we understand or accept that truth? Are we really willing to see people as they are, without judgment or bias? More importantly, are we willing to see ourselves that way?

To accept ourselves in the purest sense, we must first learn to look inward—honestly and without prejudice. That means noticing our habits, traits, and reactions simply as they are, without labeling them as "good" or "bad." For instance, if you're not a morning person, the world will likely give you endless reasons to become one. Over time, you might even make the change. But until then, that trait gets stamped as a flaw. So much so that we start believing it: "I've always been bad at waking up early."

But what if you could reframe it? What if you could say, "I started waking up early when I had to. Otherwise, I prefer sleeping in." That's it. No shame. No label. Just an honest observation of your natural rhythm.

If we can start seeing ourselves as individuals—each of us with a unique internal compass—then we can begin trusting what our bodies and minds need at any given moment. If your body needs more rest, you'll give it rest. If it needs movement, you'll move.

Take something as simple as drinking water. You might see a colleague getting up every hour to drink water on purpose, dedicatedly. While you don't have a fixed timing and you drink water only when you are thirsty. We're quick to label one behavior as healthy and the other as neglectful. But what if both are just right for the individuals practicing them? Our bodies already know when and how much water they need. When we stop comparing the litres consumed per day, we begin listening to our body. And when we listen, life becomes simpler, lighter, and far more aligned.

With this mindset, let's come to the heart of this chapter: **self-care.**

The most important relationship we will ever have is the one we have with ourselves. People, family, and friends will come and go, but we are the only constant in our lives, the ones who will face every challenge and celebrate every one of our own victories. So, it's essential to prioritize our own well-being. When we put our happiness first, we're not being selfish—we are ensuring that we are in the best position to support others and face the world with strength and grace.

To achieve this, it's essential to understand that focusing on self-care is not a luxury but a necessity. Imagine pouring from an empty cup—we can't give what we don't have. By taking care of ourselves, we fill our cups so that we can share our energy, love, and support with others and, more importantly, with ourselves.

The foundation of this care lies in the health of our physical bodies. Without good health, everything else becomes secondary. A healthy body allows us to fully experience life's pleasures, from the joy of a morning run or cup of coffee to the simple satisfaction of a good night's sleep. It's not just about aesthetics or achieving a certain look—it's about functionality, vitality, and longevity.

However, physical well-being alone is not enough; we must also nurture our mental and emotional health. Just as we wouldn't let toxic substances into our bodies, we shouldn't allow toxic people or thoughts to take root in our minds. Learn to say no to what drains you and yes to what nourishes your body and brain.

Taking time for reflection is an essential step in building mental clarity. Spend time alone—not in isolation, but in reflection. Let's really get to know ourselves. What makes us sad? What brings us joy? What makes us mad? What are our boundaries, and how can we enforce them? The more we understand ourselves, the better equipped we will be to navigate life's complexities with confidence, calmness, and clarity.

As we develop this understanding, we realize the importance of being comfortable in our own company. Being comfortable in our own company is a sign of emotional maturity. It's a reflection of a well-nurtured relationship with ourselves. And when we are content with who we are, we become a source of positivity and strength for those around us. We are not a burden to others; instead, we uplift them simply by being at peace with ourselves.

But what does it mean to be a burden? A burden is someone who, intentionally or not, strains others emotionally or physically—whether through dependence, negativity, or constant need for reassurance. When someone lacks self-confidence or isn't comfortable with who they are, they can lean too heavily on others to fill that gap. This can drain those around them, as they're often expected to keep that person's self-esteem and happiness afloat.

However, when we are secure in ourselves, the dynamic changes, and we don't rely on others for validation or support as much. This doesn't mean we don't need people—we all do—but it means we're not pulling from them out of insecurity. Instead, our presence becomes a source of strength and positivity, where we become a giver more than a receiver. We add to the well-being of those around us, offering support, joy, and calm rather than needing these things from others. We move through life with a stable sense of self, which naturally benefits those we interact with, creating a positive ripple effect.

In embracing this mindset, we take responsibility for our own happiness. This frees others from having to "fix" us or constantly meet our emotional needs. Instead of being a potential burden, we become a source of strength and encouragement, allowing our relationships to thrive without the strain of unmet expectations or emotional demands.

This concept of emotional self-sufficiency isn't just relevant to our personal lives. It applies to how we raise the next generation. Parents often prefer to see their children grow into capable individuals rather than individuals who are only capable of making money. Why? Because life experience taught the parents that success and failure are part of the human experience—and no one is immune to it either. What truly matters is having the capability to face challenges and keep moving forward, no matter what life throws at them. In other words, it's about raising emotionally self-sufficient children—people who can handle life's ups and downs without needing constant motivation or reassurance.

But how many of us are truly emotionally self-sufficient?

The good news is that becoming self-sufficient is not as difficult as we often make it. In fact, it's easier than we think. The key lies in stopping the cycle of sharing irrelevant emotional drama. How often do we find ourselves caught up in the urge to unload our inner turmoil, thoughts, or minor frustrations onto others? We're driven by the need to have someone else know exactly what we're thinking or feeling at any given moment—yet much of that emotional drama is fleeting and ultimately insignificant.

If you're wondering how much of this drama truly matters, it's worth reflecting on the past. Consider this: How much time have we spent rehashing, editing, or directing our emotional "drama," convincing ourselves that it needs to be shared? If you ever wonder how irrelevant it is, ask yourself "what were you preoccupied with five years ago"? Chances are, you won't even remember the details of those thoughts, yet at that moment, they probably felt like the most essential thing in your world.

Let's be honest: the people who call us, supposedly checking in on how we're feeling, often aren't really interested in listening. They're simply waiting for our story to end so they can unload their own emotional baggage. It's an unspoken mutual agreement—both parties help each other offload their drama, and if it's not given the attention it craves, another round of drama is bound to follow within a day or two. We're stuck in this cycle, but we fail to recognize how irrelevant these emotional exchanges really are. Not only do they drain our energy, but they also distort our thinking, making it harder to stay grounded and focused.

It's similar to when a friend introduces us to a new brand or logo—suddenly, we start noticing it everywhere. In the same way, the emotional drama we exchange begins to seep into every part of our lives. We get used to it, because it becomes our reference point. We start to notice it, discuss it, and invest time and energy into it without realizing we're just feeding the cycle.

Remember the saying, "Garbage in, garbage out?" These constant exchanges of emotional noise can leave us feeling more exhausted, less clear-headed, and disconnected from ourselves. It's crucial to protect our energy, recognize when these interactions are no longer serving us, and practice discernment in what we allow to take root in our minds.

The key to emotional self-sufficiency lies in recognizing and choosing not to feed into that drama. When we identify our emotional drama and decide not to give it the time and energy it craves, we begin to take control of our own well-being. We stop the cycle of unnecessary emotional sharing and start prioritizing more productive habits. Refusing to indulge in drama creates space for growth and emotional maturity.

This process—of choosing not to feed our emotional chaos—is a powerful form of self-care. It allows us to preserve our energy and focus on what truly matters, enabling us to be more resilient, more at peace, and better able to navigate life's challenges without leaning too heavily on others for support.

In the corporate world, self-care isn't just a personal need —it's a professional requirement. A person who neglects his well-being is like a car running on empty; sooner or later, it will break down or stop abruptly. When we care for ourselves, we are better equipped to manage our responsibilities, meet deadlines, and contribute meaningfully to our customers and team. Our productivity, creativity, and resilience all stem from a foundation of a good state of mind, which can't be obtained without a healthy body.

Remember, no one else can care for us as well as we can. Prioritizing our health, setting boundaries, and ensuring we have time to recharge are essential for our personal happiness and professional success.

CHAPTER 10

GRASS IS GREENER ON THE OTHER SIDE

We've all heard the saying, "The grass is always greener on the other side." It's a total cliche phrase that captures how we often view others' lives as more desirable, fulfilling, or somehow better than our own. We look at the people we admire—our role models, friends, celebrities, politicians, successful business people— and imagine that they have it all figured out. But the truth is, everyone has their own share of struggles and challenges. No one is immune to life's ups and downs.

Let's take an example - Hollywood celebrities or top athletes. From the outside, their lives seem like pure glitz and glamor, but they deal with the same struggles we all face behind the scenes. Whether it's health issues, relationship troubles, or personal/professional setbacks, these are just part of being human. Yet, we don't often see this side of their lives because social media and public appearances are carefully curated to show only the most positive filtered aspects. It's like a brand-building exercise, where the reality is often hidden behind a carefully crafted image.

We must remember that a simple thing like a cold or a bad day can knock anyone off balance. That's how delicate and unpredictable life is for everyone, no matter who they are. We assume that someone like an artist or a musician lives a more enjoyable life because they are immersed in their craft/expertise. We see a painter lost in creating a beautiful landscape and assume they're in a constant state of bliss. But in reality, they are just as human as the rest of us, dealing with the same mundane tasks and everyday frustrations. It's about finding those moments of joy and focus amidst the everyday grind.

We also experience moments of deep focus and enjoyment in our lives. Still, we often miss seeing them because they don't seem as glamorous. Whether it's writing an important email, preparing a presentation, getting immersed in a good book, cooking a meal, or even something as simple as cleaning your home, these are moments where we are fully engaged. We might not recognize their value because society places a higher status on artistic endeavors like painting or music. However, that doesn't mean our experiences are less satisfying or meaningful.

For example, listening to music can be as fulfilling as playing an instrument. If you have a keen ear and appreciate the intricacies of a piece of music, you might get more joy from listening than someone else does from playing. It's all about perspective. We must break the myth that artists or certain professions enjoy life more than others. Sure, they might have their moments, but so do we. Happiness isn't reserved for the few and isn't associated with specific crafts —it's available to anyone who finds joy in everyday moments.

Suppose we allow ourselves to be genuinely involved in our lives. In that case, we don't need grand plans or extravagant activities to be happy. Even the simplest chores can be satisfying if we approach them with the right mindset. Why can't we enjoy brushing teeth, ironing clothes, showering, or gardening? Why do we associate cleanliness with obsessive-compulsive disorder instead of seeing it as a beautiful habit of maintaining a clean and healthy living space? We shouldn't let labels define us or dictate how we view our actions. If you enjoy keeping your home tidy, embrace that and feel good about it. It's not a syndrome; it's a part of who you are.

We are all unique in our ways, and we don't have to fit neatly into categories like introvert or extrovert. It's okay if we don't conform to society's labels. Let society come up with new terms if they must, but we don't need to live our lives justifying any tag. Let's just be who we are, finding happiness in our own way, without comparing ourselves to others or needing to live up to some external standard. Happiness is about finding joy in the ordinary and appreciating the extraordinary moments when they happen.

We've all been there—scrolling through social media, seeing friends or influencers living what looks like the perfect life. They're off on exotic vacations, showing off luxurious homes, or posting about their picture-perfect relationships.

It's easy to feel like our own lives are falling short. But let's be honest: we don't see the arguments that happened just before that flawless photo, the debt propping up that lavish lifestyle, or the loneliness behind those smiles. Social media is nothing but a highlight reel; it doesn't tell the whole story.

Take career success, for example. You might admire a CEO for their wealth and power, thinking they've got it all. But what's hidden behind that success? The constant pressure, the long hours, the personal sacrifices—missing family dinners, not having time for friends, and carrying the weight of an entire company on their shoulders and being answerable to multiple stakeholders. While we're busy thinking their life is better, they might wish for the simplicity of a weekend spent with family, free from stress.

Parenting and family life can also be a classic case of "the grass is greener." You might see another family and think they've got it all together—well-behaved kids, a spotless home, and a picture-perfect family dynamic. But let's not forget that every family has struggles, whether dealing with tantrums, juggling work and parenting, or keeping a marriage strong. That image of the "perfect family" is just that—an image.

And what about those who seem to be in peak physical condition? It's easy to admire someone fit and healthy, assuming their life must be easier because of it. But we often don't see the early morning workouts, the strict diets, and the sacrifices they make to stay in shape. Even then, they're not immune to health issues, injuries, or the same body insecurities we all face.

Finally, there's financial security. We might envy someone with a bigger house, a nicer car, or a more prestigious job, thinking their wealth brings them happiness. But financial stability often comes with its own pressures—the fear of losing it all, the burden of keeping up appearances, and the isolation that can come from working long hours to sustain it. Meanwhile, someone with less might find joy in simpler things and have a stronger sense of community and connection.

CHAPTER 11

FUNCTIONAL FITNESS AND HAPPINESS

Broadly, there are two kinds of fitness: functional and what many call gym fitness. But what exactly do we mean by functional fitness? Functional fitness refers to exercises and activities that improve our ability to perform everyday tasks—like bending down to pick up something, carrying shopping bags, or playing with our children. It's about strengthening the muscles we use in daily life, rather than focusing solely on aesthetics or specific muscle groups. This type of fitness emphasizes mobility, strength, endurance, and flexibility—all the physical attributes that help us move through life with ease and without discomfort.

But have you ever wondered how our belief system around fitness was formed? For most of us, being able to get out of bed easily, complete daily chores without strain, walk a mile, or take the stairs instead of the elevator isn't even seen as part of being fit. These simple actions are either taken for granted or not paid attention to until we struggle to perform any of them.

Let's take a moment to reflect: When was the last time we appreciated our bodies for getting us through the day without discomfort? Maybe it was when we carried groceries up the stairs without feeling winded or when we decided to walk a mile extra to challenge our limits. These functional abilities allow us to live our life fully, which otherwise can stop us from leading a happy life.

Today, however, fitness has become associated with appearance—having a broad chest, big arms, and sculpted legs. We spend hours in the gym trying to build muscle, supplementing our diets with pre- and post-workout shakes, all in pursuit of a particular look. But in focusing on this, we overlook the real gift: our body's natural ability to function efficiently, which supports us in living well. Instead, we mold our bodies into the image that marketing and advertising industries want us to chase, which keeps a whole sector thriving. At the same time, we miss out on the happiness of simply being able to move, breathe, and live.

Think about how often we say things like, "I feel amazing on chest workout day," or "Leg day gives me such a high." This mindset creates a pattern of tying our happiness to specific workouts or achieving a particular physique. But what happens on days when we don't go to the gym or don't feel like working out? We feel a sense of guilt by the end of the day. This guilt comes from the preconditions we have set for ourselves. Our happiness becomes conditional—dependent on reaching a temporary goal. This is like saving happiness for some future version of ourselves while missing out on being happy right now.

Consider a real-world example: imagine ourselves as parents, spending our days chasing after our children, lifting them, playing with them, and carrying them to bed. We might not go to the gym, but our bodies are strong and capable of supporting us in the most important job of our lives. This is functional fitness in action. Shouldn't we feel proud and happy for our strength and agility rather than pressured to fit into a specific "gym-fit" mold? This doesn't mean there's anything wrong with going to the gym. But there's a key difference between exercising for health and exercising to achieve an image that society glorifies. Before setting goals for a bigger chest or toned abs, we need to learn to appreciate and be happy with our bodies as they are. A fit body doesn't need to look a certain way; it needs to support us in living our lives. Otherwise, we're postponing our happiness—chasing a moving target. What if societal standards change again by the time we achieve our "ideal" body? We'd find ourselves in an endless cycle of chasing someone else's idea of fitness, always just one step away from happiness.

Let's stop being driven by these campaigns. Instead, let's accept our bodies for what they can do now and use them regularly to keep them active. We should aim to be better versions of ourselves, not reflections of a marketing campaign. Physical activity is an integral part of life, but it should enhance our lives, not become the sole purpose of it.

Our bodies communicate with the world. If we're lazy, we don't have to announce it—our bodies will show it. If we're active, our bodies advertise that too. Think of someone who can walk long distances without feeling winded or someone who can easily squat to lift a heavy box. Our bodies reflect functional strength, not just gym-built muscles. This kind of fitness is far more enduring and brings lasting happiness because it's about capability, not image.

Let's focus on functional fitness first. Can we climb a ladder if needed? Can we stand in a long line or lift our hands above our head without discomfort? Can we enjoy cooking a meal without needing to sit down? These are the types of fitness that truly matter in our day-to-day lives. When we can move through our daily routines without struggle, we should celebrate that. It's the kind of fitness that supports a whole life—and that's where our happiness lies.

When was the last time life demanded that you run a marathon? The answer, for most of us, is probably "never." Now, think about this: when was the last time you had to lift 100 pounds in a real-life situation? Again, you might be struggling to recall. In fact, most of us don't face these extreme physical challenges in our day-to-day lives. Yet, we continue to train as if life is constantly testing our endurance, pushing us to stretch our limits, and trying to make us fitter, faster, and stronger. But why? To look good? To appear leaner or more muscular than the next person?

Of course, leading an active life is valuable. But what about when we get caught in the cycle of pushing ourselves too hard? Addiction to intense workouts and striving for goals that don't necessarily serve our immediate needs or happiness can take a toll. Sometimes, we forget that resting—allowing ourselves to be still—is just as essential for our well-being.

In fact, there's something incredibly nourishing about lying on the couch or in bed every once in a while—doing nothing, worrying about nothing, and planning nothing. If you ever find yourself in that peaceful state, let yourself remain there as long as possible. Believe it or not, those moments of complete relaxation might be doing more for you than any workout ever could.

When we rest deeply, our bodies release chemicals that help us feel at ease. Not everyone experiences these moments of release, and not everyone gives themselves permission to be still long enough to allow these chemicals to do their work. But when we do, our immune systems get a boost, and our minds find peace.

As the saying goes, "Whatever you're doing, you're getting good at it." In this case, when you allow yourself to experience and enjoy true relaxation, you're actually getting better at being at ease. And just like you might practice a morning stretch to ensure your body moves smoothly throughout the day, moments of actual stillness can help you build a sense of calm and peace that can be carried with you. Over time, this ease becomes an integral part of who you are—your personality—allowing you to live in a state of greater balance.

Take a moment to consider this: while a brisk walk, jog, or run can be great for your heart and blood circulation, the key is not to turn these simple, beneficial activities into an act of self-punishment. Many people wake up with a mission to run an extra mile or lift a few extra pounds, pushing themselves to compete against their physical limitations. And why? Because somewhere, someone told them, "When the going gets tough, the tough get going." Or maybe it was the mantra, "no pain, no gain."

So, before reaching the breakfast table, we've already been battling ourselves.We've chosen to fight against our own physical limitations before the real battles of the day even begin. And by the time we head out the door, we're already running on empty, fatigued from the effort we put into our workout.

This is where functional fitness comes in. The point of fitness isn't to punish ourselves but to equip our bodies to serve us better daily. Yes, a good workout or sport involving ample physical movements and pulling and stretching muscles helps release endorphins in our body. Still, we should also appreciate the moments of relaxation where our body works quietly to re-energize ourselves. Instead of chasing an ever-elusive "ideal" body, let's focus on developing a body that serves us—strong enough to carry us through our daily tasks, agile enough to navigate our environment without struggle, and significantly peaceful enough to appreciate life as it unfolds.

Remember, life doesn't demand a six-pack or bulging biceps; it demands functional fitness. The ability to move freely, bend down to tie our shoes, climb stairs without huffing and puffing, or easily carry groceries. These are the true markers of fitness, and they're the ones that bring us lasting happiness—because they allow us to live life fully without constantly feeling that we need to measure up to some external standard of beauty or strength.

Think about what has shaped our ideas of fitness. Is it the movie stars with their shirtless photos fresh out of the gym or the models on fitness magazine covers? These images shape what we think fitness should look like but rarely represent what it feels like. Real fitness is about feeling good in our bodies, having the energy to do what we love, and finding joy in our physical capabilities—no matter how they look.

CHAPTER 12

ACCUMULATION – HOW MUCH IS Enough?

One of the biggest sources of stress today is the lack of time and energy to pursue what truly makes us happy. Yet, we often encounter people who seem to have mastered the art of doing what brings them joy. How do they manage it? The key lies in introspection. But how can we introspect without first sitting down and evaluating where our time and energy are going? After all, every person has the same 24 hours in a day. So why do we feel so drained?

A good starting point is to sit alone and look at how we spend our time daily. What consumes most of our energy? Unsurprisingly, for many of us, the answer lies in one thing: accumulation. After tending to basic needs like sleep, food, and some exercise, most of us quickly shift into a relentless cycle of gathering more—whether that's money, knowledge, or social status.

Take students as an example. They might spend hours cramming for exams, not out of passion for learning but out of the need to pass tests and accumulate grades. Or consider a professional who spends extra hours at the office, not because they love their work, but because they need the paycheck. Then there's the socialite who's constantly working on building connections, not for friendship, but to accumulate status and validation. In all these cases, the goal is never-ending, which leads to burnout and a sense of emptiness.

We all invest time and energy into what we believe is essential. But how deeply are we driven by these pursuits? That's where things diverge. Some people find passion in the process. They love their work or studies and look forward to each day. We've all known students who are enthusiastic about their subjects or colleagues who thrive in their jobs. But for every passionate person, there's someone else merely going through the motions—working for a paycheck, keeping busy, or just fulfilling a societal role or to accumulate more money and wealth.

If we are not passionate about our work, we must ask ourselves: How much do I need? What exactly am I chasing, and how long will this chase go on? The clarity that comes from answering these questions can reduce stress. Our path becomes clearer once we understand why we are doing what we are doing and how long we intend to keep doing it. Each of us is on our own journey. Still, ambiguity about that journey often leads to anxiety—unless, of course, we are someone who is unfazed by life's unpredictability.

We often find ourselves caught in the endless cycle of working tirelessly to accumulate wealth, constantly striving for the next promotion or higher title in pursuit of more income and stability. Our plans for happiness are frequently postponed to a vague "someday"—a distant retirement where we imagine finally enjoying the fruits of our labor. But how do we determine when we've saved or earned enough? Why don't we take a moment to enjoy earning and living in the present? The future is uncertain, and the wealth we accumulate today is never guaranteed. Investments can be unpredictable, and financial crises can affect anyone—even millionaires are not immune. Beyond the unpredictability of finances, how can we be sure we will be physically capable of enjoying what we've worked so hard to achieve? Instead of placing happiness on hold for an uncertain future, why not embrace the wealth we already have—both material and intangible—and find contentment in the here and now?

Think of it like packing for a trip. We only take the essentials because carrying extra weight makes the journey harder. Similarly, why carry unnecessary burdens if our job isn't our passion? Cut down on expenses and unnecessary indulgences to reach our financial goals faster. By streamlining our lives, we create space to figure out what truly makes us happy and ultimately escape an environment that drains us. Financial stability begins with mindful spending, but how many of us actually realize when we've accumulated enough? We often fall into the trap of wanting more—to impress others, satisfy societal pressures, or give our kids a lifestyle we never had. This becomes a vicious cycle, where we get caught up in responsibilities towards family, colleagues, or society, losing sight of our happiness.

Let's not forget the digital world. Accumulation isn't limited to money and possessions—it extends to social media. We see people obsessively collecting likes, followers, or comments, mistaking digital approval for real-life fulfillment. But no number of likes can replace genuine relationships. The more we chase these intangible forms of validation, the more we lose touch with ourselves.

Let's look at three ways to help break the cycle of accumulation.

Breaking the Cycle: Three Steps to Freedom

1.) Stop doing the wrong things

We often accumulate far more than we need, convinced it will bring happiness. But emotional attachment to this process, without realizing the stress it causes, leads us further away from joy.

Example: Think of someone who buys the latest smartphone every year, not because their old one stopped working, but to stay "ahead" of others. The temporary satisfaction fades away quickly, but the habit continues, leaving them in constant dissatisfaction

2.) Start doing the right things

Recognize that material things are meant to enhance life, not dominate it. They should not be the focus of every waking moment.

Example: Imagine a family downsizing to a smaller home. Initially, it feels like a sacrifice, but over time, they find more time for meaningful activities and connections because they no longer need to keep up with the maintenance and costs of a larger house.

3.) Reap the rewards of your choices

Once you're out of the cycle, you'll feel a newfound sense of freedom. You're no longer chasing wealth or status but living for yourself. Every effort goes into enhancing your life experience rather than proving your worth to an employer or society.

Example: Someone who leaves a high-stress corporate job to pursue a passion project might earn less, but they feel more fulfilled, have more time, and live with far less stress. They've gained a deeper sense of satisfaction by prioritizing personal happiness over societal measures of success.

Each step toward this freedom brings a sense of calm. We don't have to wait until we have reached the final stage to notice a difference. Even the first step—consciously reducing unnecessary accumulation—can be transformative. It allows us to breathe and take stock of what really matters.

When it comes to raising children, our responsibility should not be to give them every luxury imaginable. Instead, let's focus on raising thoughtful, capable, and kind human beings. We must understand that our children don't need to be replicas of ourselves, just as we are not identical to our parents. Each child is a unique individual, and our role is to equip them for life as it truly is, not shield them with endless material comforts.

If we succeed in this, we won't need to worry about their future. They'll be smart enough—perhaps smarter than us—to navigate life's ups and downs. But if we raise them in an environment where luxuries come first, we risk making them dependent, not just on us but on society. And that, ultimately, is a disservice to both them and the world around them.

Accumulation without purpose is a road to nowhere. We can spend our lives chasing material wealth, social validation, or experiences that leave us hollow. But what's the point of working hard if you can't enjoy life along the way? The true wealth we should seek is the ability to live in harmony with our values, find fulfillment in small moments, and free ourselves from the relentless pursuit of "more." Life is short, and the real reward isn't found in what we accumulate but in how we experience it.

The journey toward simplicity and mindfulness isn't always easy. Still, its peace is worth far more than any material gain. Start today by asking yourself what truly matters—and let go of the rest.

Offer food to an animal, and it will eat its fill. Give it more, and while it may indulge a bit, once it's satisfied, it stops. Animals don't demand beyond their needs. Think of a dog—no matter how much food you leave out, it will eat until full and walk away, content with what's in its belly. It doesn't store extra food for later or worry about what tomorrow will bring. But humans—uniquely—don't seem to know when to stop. We constantly want more than we can eat, wear, consume, or hold onto. Why? Because we can store and hoard.

The real question becomes: How much do we need to store? And more importantly, what are we storing, and is it bringing peace or ease into our lives? For instance, our closet. How many clothes do we actually wear compared to what's stored away? We accumulate outfits for 'someday,' yet most hang untouched for months, gathering dust. If what we already have hasn't given us contentment, what makes us believe that having more will suddenly create happiness?

In our society, there's always someone with more than we have and always someone with less. The strange part is that we all want a little more regardless of where we fall on that spectrum. The person with less wants what we have, and we want what someone with more possesses. The cycle is endless. It's like being on a treadmill, constantly running toward a goal but never arriving. Whether it's that new car, the bigger house, or the next promotion, once we have it, we'll stop. But we don't. We admire the lives of others because they have what we don't, while they, in turn, look up to someone else. It's a perpetual game of "if only" — if only

I had that job, that partner, that house, that bank balance, then I'd be happy.

This mindset keeps contentment always just out of reach in some distant future. We spend so much of life chasing this "if," never realizing that we're preconditioning our happiness on something external. As a result, we rarely pause to notice what we have right now. Consider the act of eating a meal. Instead of savoring each bite, we often think about what's next—dessert, the next meal, or the following chores. We rarely allow ourselves to fully enjoy the moment.

Take a moment to think about it. How often do you feel uneasy saying, "I don't know"? We are reluctant to admit ignorance because society has taught us that admitting a lack of knowledge makes us seem out of touch, old, or unimportant. It's not just about being uninformed—it's about the fear of losing our social status or image. To avoid this discomfort, we continuously accumulate information and knowledge to stay "up to date," even when that chase becomes exhausting. Picture the endless consumption of news, social media, and online updates. We fear being left behind, even when all this knowledge leaves us anxious and overwhelmed. This endless need for more information keeps us in a mental rat race, all in the name of protecting our image.

Similarly, the fear of saying, "I don't have," is deeply tied to our insecurities. It's not just about lacking material things; it's about what that lack represents. To say, "I don't have," suggests we've failed—failed to be smart enough, hardworking enough, or resourceful enough to get what we want. Even if we don't openly judge others for having less, we often think they haven't tried as hard. Take the way we might view someone driving an old car or wearing outdated clothes—we usually assume their lack of success stems from laziness or poor choices, even if that's far from the truth. Yet, when we encounter someone wealthier, we attribute their success to luck, never questioning our own intelligence. Isn't it ironic that our intelligence is never the problem when we look upward but always the explanation when we look down?

The truth is intelligence isn't measured by the numbers in our bank account or the abundance of things we possess. Rather, accurate intelligence is directly proportional to the ease of life we lead ourselves and the ease we bring to the lives of others. Let's use our smartness to create a more meaningful life—where our actions and intentions make us an asset to those around us, not a liability to society, burdened by an insatiable desire for more. Intelligence is about living simply yet richly without needing to conquer the never-ending urge for a little more.

Imagine living with a sense of contentment—like an animal that stops eating when it's full. Recognizing that happiness doesn't come from having more but from appreciating what we already have is the true art of living in the present. Reflect on the satisfaction of completing a small task—like organizing a drawer or finishing a good book. These moments of accomplishment often bring a more profound sense of joy and fulfillment than acquiring another gadget or piece of clothing ever could.

This isn't about depriving ourselves but realizing that happiness isn't tied to excess. It's about saying, "I have enough," and indeed mean it. Picture someone who has just finished decluttering their home, removing all the unnecessary items that once filled their space. The newfound sense of clarity and peace that follows is a testament to the power of living with less.

Humans tend to hoard, constantly wanting more—food, knowledge, or possessions. Society fuels this by keeping us in a state of comparison, where we always strive for what others have. But this pursuit leaves us unsatisfied because contentment is never found in a future "if only."

True happiness comes from recognizing when enough is enough. By focusing on the present and contributing meaningfully to the world around us, we can free ourselves from the endless chase for more and fully appreciate the life we already have.

CHAPTER 13

PROFESSIONAL VS PERSONAL PROBLEM SOLVING

At work, solving problems is a well-defined process. We're trained to approach challenges precisely, following a logical sequence of steps we've mastered over time. In a professional setting, we may even be the person everyone turns to for solutions - the pro. We've built a reputation through years of practice, applying structured methods like brainstorming, root cause analysis, or agile frameworks. We can quickly outline every step of our process and predict potential pitfalls. In short, when it comes to problem-solving at work, we excel.

The corporate world trains us to "identify the problem" as the first step. Whether it's handling a product launch delay or resolving team conflicts, we know how to break down complex issues and turn them into manageable tasks. We create action plans, assign responsibilities, track progress, and eventually solve the problem. But when we step outside the workplace and face challenges in our personal lives, all of this professional expertise seems to disappear.

Where does all this technical expertise disappear when confronted with a real-life issue? Why do we fail to apply this systematic approach to our personal lives? Take an example from work: you're tasked with managing a project over budget and behind schedule. You immediately start by assessing the situation, identifying the issues, and rallying the team to develop solutions. You communicate the problem to stakeholders, break the project into smaller pieces, and devise a plan to get back on track.

Consider a common personal life situation—constant misunderstandings with your partner. Instead of taking the time to identify what's really causing the friction, we often let emotions take over. Instead of articulating the issue, we feel overwhelmed and shut down, or worse, we assign blame. While we might quickly confront a problem at work, we delay difficult conversations at home, convincing ourselves that things will eventually work out on their own. The professional logic somehow feels out of reach in these emotional situations.

Or look at our ability to deal with difficult colleagues versus difficult personal relationships. At work, if you have a high-spirited boss who lacks strategic thinking, you could address this by focusing on facts, laying out a plan, and managing expectations. In contrast, in a romantic relationship, we may start questioning the relationship itself instead of problem-solving when the initial spark fades. We often dwell in confusion, wondering why things aren't like they used to be, rather than identifying the problem clearly: perhaps we've stopped communicating as effectively as we once did.

The same goes for friendships. Imagine a close friend whose sense of humor no longer aligned with yours. Instead of addressing the shift, you might laugh along to maintain harmony, all while feeling disconnected. At work, you wouldn't hesitate to give feedback if a colleague's approach was no longer practical, so why do we hold back in personal life?

When real-life problems arise, rather than approaching them with clear thinking, we get caught in endless loops of overthinking. A simple event, like a loved one not responding to a message, can spiral into an emotional drama. We craft imaginary scenarios in our head—perhaps they're mad at us, maybe we've done something wrong—and our emotions react to these hypothetical situations as if they were real.

Could you think of the mental energy we waste? For instance, after a minor disagreement with a partner, we might spend hours replaying the conversation, imagining everything we should have said. These things trigger a never-ending drama in our heads, and the permutation combinations are unlimited. We can continue creating hypothetical situations in our minds and simultaneously emotionally responding to them all. When we've exhausted ourselves with these hypothetical arguments, we say, "I need to sleep on it," or "I need a break." But sleep doesn't solve the issue, nor does taking a break, because we haven't applied the same problem-solving skills we would in a work setting. These are the efforts called 'buying oats for a dead horse,' i.e., a complete waste of energy on what feels like solving a problem, but in reality, we've been chasing imaginary scenarios.

Consider how much clarity we could gain if we applied the professional logic we use at work. Instead of mentally exhausting ourselves with "what-ifs," we could identify the actual problem: maybe the disagreement arose because we felt unheard or because of stress outside the relationship. Once the problem is clear, it becomes easier to solve.

The key question is: why do we treat our personal life problems so differently from work problems? One reason might be that personal issues feel more ambiguous. Problems are often external at work, and we are trained to fix them.

In our personal lives, the issues feel closer to home, messier, and more entangled with our emotions, so we accept them as part of life rather than problems to solve. We have unknowingly made an agreement with ourselves that professional issues require solutions while personal issues require acceptance. But why? When did we decide that personal challenges weren't worth addressing with the same precision? In our personal life, we often don't even get to the first step of problem-solving: identifying the problem. Imagine you're feeling distant from a partner. Instead of thinking clearly about why that distance exists, you might label it as "relationship problems" and leave it at that. But a vague label doesn't offer a path forward. What if you treated it like a work issue? You'd ask questions to define the problem more clearly: "Are we not spending enough time together?" "Has communication broken down?" With a precise problem statement, you can start moving toward a solution, whether it's scheduling quality time together or improving communication.

This doesn't just apply to relationships. Think about personal finances. If you notice your spending is out of control, instead of saying, "I'm bad with money," and feeling stuck, you can take a work-based approach: track your spending, identify patterns, and set goals. The moment you get clear on the problem, you're halfway to solving it.

The reality is that the same principles we apply at work can help us find clarity and solutions in our personal lives. By taking the time to identify the specific problem, we can move past the vague labels and emotional turmoil and into a space where solutions are possible. Imagine treating personal conflicts like a project at work: start by identifying the problem, brainstorm potential solutions, and take concrete steps to address it. The process is the same—only the context is different.

Once again, our inability to clearly define the problem is often the biggest challenge—not because we're incapable, but because we're not in the habit of doing so. Try this simple exercise the next time you're stressed: instead of juggling the thoughts in your head, take out a pen and paper (or use your laptop) and start writing. Begin with the sentence, "I'm stressed because…" and then explain. Don't hold back. Pour out everything that's causing the stress.

Write in detail. Pause if you need to, and re-read what you've written. Does it make sense? If not, edit it until it feels right or flows in a logical order. Keep explaining until you've fully vented everything preventing you from being a happier version of yourself.

Let's say you're stressed because you disagreed with a friend. Your mind races with everything you wish you'd said or done differently. Instead of letting those thoughts swirl endlessly, write: "I'm stressed because I feel misunderstood. I didn't explain my point during our conversation, and now I'm worried they're upset with me." As you continue writing, you might uncover deeper layers of the problem—maybe it's not just this conversation that's bothering you, but a pattern of communication over time.

Remember, this is your story—your version of events. No one else needs to see it. There are no external judges, no counter-arguments, no filters. Just the raw, unfiltered truth from your perspective. This level of honesty is crucial for the exercise to work. Suppose you can commit to doing this with 100% honesty. In that case, you'll notice that the issues causing you stress will often start to disappear even before you finish writing about them. Why? Because you've given yourself permission to express how you feel without self-editing or second-guessing.

But how does this actually work? Why does writing about our stress lead to such relief?

Think of it this way: when we write, we tend to follow a logical sequence. Our thoughts are naturally more structured, and we stay focused on the core issue. In contrast, when we think, our minds often wander in a zig-zag pattern. We get easily distracted, either by other thoughts or by our surroundings. We frequently return to the same thought repeatedly but with varying intensities, rehashing the problem without ever resolving it.

Imagine trying to finish a puzzle while someone keeps handing us new pieces every few seconds. We'd never be able to focus on completing the original puzzle! That's what it's like when we try to "think" through stress. We know where to go, but we take too long to get there because our thoughts keep looping back in endless variations.

When we write, however, we approach the issue more structured. As we continue writing, the distractions fall away, and we move closer to the heart of the matter.

Another possible outcome of this exercise is that we will gain amazing clarity about the issue we are dealing with. Broadly speaking, there are two kinds of problems:

- Issues we can control (e.g., things within our sphere of influence, like managing our schedule or improving a skill).

- Issues we can't control (e.g., external factors beyond our control, like someone else's behavior or unpredictable events).

Imagine you're worried about an upcoming work presentation. You may realize that what's stressing you out is within your control—like not feeling fully prepared. In that case, the solution is to spend more time practicing. But let's say the stress comes from fear that your boss will respond negatively, something out of your control. Recognizing this is beyond your influence can give you peace of mind, as you're no longer burdened with trying to change something you cannot.

Either way, having clarity on which type of issue we face provides our brain with much-needed relief from the endless mental loops that generate stress. Our brains are wired to understand logic. Once our brain clearly registers, "This is something I can't control," it stops stressing over it. The act of accepting what's beyond our control allows our minds to rest. We'll notice that the stress dissipates simply because our brain now accepts that it can't solve what's out of its hands.

CHAPTER 14

AGING AND HAPPINESS

It all started from our desperation. As kids, we couldn't wait to grow up; once we grew up, we couldn't wait to become financially independent. Then, it was about landing a better job or project. Next came the desire for the perfect life partner and the longing to be free of that partner for some of us. Some of us even calculate how much we need for the rest of our lives, chasing that figure like it's an insurance policy.

Sometimes, we look back at our lives and think, "Growing up was fun," indirectly suggesting that it's not fun anymore. Ever wondered why?

It's only because we are not accustomed to being at ease in the present moment. As grown-ups, if we find ourselves at ease, we often feel like we're not doing enough. Grown-ups must be occupied—whether in the relentless pursuit of money, acquiring new skills for future earnings, or executing various plans. We juggle numerous targets simultaneously, so ingrained in this idea of planning that we can't function without it.

Consider a college student preparing for finals. They're caught up in the grind, juggling study sessions, part-time work, and social obligations. They've created a meticulous schedule to ensure they cover every topic. However, in their quest for perfection, they often forget to take breaks and enjoy simple pleasures—like a sunny day or a spontaneous outing with friends. They remain engrossed in accumulating knowledge and achievements. Still, they feel compelled to do something for society once they've reached their goals. And guess what? That, too, requires planning and execution.

Do we even realize that many of us would freak out if we woke up on a Monday morning with nothing substantial on our to-do list instead of feeling blessed? This is because we are not used to living without a grand plan; every minute spent without an urge to do something feels wasted. The idea of pausing to take stock of where we're heading and why we're heading there is often overshadowed by societal norms that dictate our actions. We don't have time for these thoughts.

We often hear phrases like, "Live life to the fullest." But what does that mean? Different people have different definitions. For some, it might mean making as much money as possible. For a single person, it may involve dating as many people as possible. An alcoholic might interpret it as gulping down as many drinks as possible. At the same time, a traveler could equate it to visiting as many destinations as possible. For an adrenaline junkie, it might mean driving as fast as possible or trying one adventure sport after another.

However, the essence of living fully is about understanding the phase of life one goes through and ensuring that we don't miss out on experiences unique to that phase. We don't want to get old and wonder why we didn't take advantage of our youth.

In our younger years, we had an unlimited energy supply, allowing us to dive into any activity that crossed our path. But as we grow older, we become more energy-conscious, carefully choosing where to spend our time and effort. This is part of maturing with age. While we may not have the same energy levels we once did, we have gained intelligence and a wealth of information.

The real question is: Are we using this intelligence to evaluate our lives, or has someone else hired our intellect for a price we believe adds to our societal value? If it's the latter, rest assured that someone will exploit every ounce of your energy, keeping you so occupied that you'll never have the chance to introspect. And if you find time on a weekend or during a flight, you'll likely be too exhausted to act on any insights you gain. Add family responsibilities into the mix, and introspection feels like a distant dream.

We risk becoming well-programmed robots, working tirelessly in our respective industries to remain relevant. Time and tide wait for none. Before we know it, a lifetime has passed, and we've spent it on pursuits that no longer excite us.

Let me share a secret: if you visit a nursing home, you'll encounter various faces telling different stories. Look closely, and you'll see the same faces that once radiated vitality now wear expressions of disappointment and regret. Their health, once their most significant asset, has dwindled, and everything they thought was essential now seems unworthy of the effort they put in. They've learned this lesson too late, leaving them with a continuous sense of grievance.

Yet, in the same nursing home, you may encounter a few smiling faces—those who never took anything too seriously. They are the ones who figured out long back, what needed to be done and why. Hence, they are free from any emotional drama. They share life's hidden secrets, often wrapped in sarcasm. They have no complaints and continue to find humor in their surroundings, even where others struggle to appreciate the color of the walls.

We have all been blessed with what it takes to live fully, but we must pause and introspect regularly. External factors and societal pressures will continue to knock on our doors, whether we like it or not. The crucial question is: How much of it can we let influence our lives?

The parameter is simple: no plan is more significant than the life we've been blessed with. If a plan stops you from focusing on your life first, it's not worth pursuing.

Ultimately, the essence of truly living lies not in the endless pursuit of achievements or societal approval but in the simple act of living life now. It's about finding joy in the mundane, cherishing the fleeting moments, and embracing the uncertainty of life without the pressure of a grand plan. As we navigate this journey, let us remember that our worth isn't defined by our accomplishments but by our ability to appreciate each day as it comes. So, pause, breathe, and embrace the beauty of now—because the most fulfilling life is not meticulously scripted but one that is lived wholeheartedly in the moment.

CHAPTER 15

THE POWER OF ENOUGH

One of the primary sources of stress in our lives comes from the gap between reality and expectation. Instead of being happy or content with what we have, we often direct our energy toward what we believe we should have. This cycle has become so ingrained in our daily lives that it's like our second nature. We constantly strive for more—more success, more money, more recognition—and we think that "enough" is always just a little out of reach. But the truth is, we rarely stop to question this drive. Whether our goals are "realistic" or "unrealistic," we are caught in an endless chase for something—a purpose, a passion, or a feeling of fulfillment—that we think will make us feel complete and alive.

Have we ever paused to take a step back from this constant pursuit? Have we ever taken a day to enjoy what we have accumulated so far, whether it's wealth, relationships, or achievements? Too often, we go through life not appreciating what we have but constantly pushing ourselves toward what we think we should have. We keep working towards the next promotion, the next significant milestone, or the next "must-have" in our lives. And the truth is, we seldom give ourselves permission to stop.

Think about a typical day at home. Have you ever had a day where you didn't need to reorganize the closet, deep clean the house, or complete a personal project but still felt the urge to do so? We are so accustomed to staying busy, to filling every moment with "productive" tasks, that we forget how to enjoy the space we've already created. Even during weekends, we often push ourselves to keep ticking off tasks on our to-do lists, missing the opportunity to just be. In these moments, we forget that rest and relaxation are productive, too.

Now, consider a holiday or a trip to a favorite destination. What makes those moments so unique? One primary reason is that, during those times, we aren't chasing anything. Our minds are free from the pressure of future demands, and we can fully immerse ourselves in the present moment. We feel that our time away is earned—we've worked hard for this break, and it's well-deserved. This sense of accomplishment allows us to relax and enjoy the now without the nagging thought of "what's next." It's a space where we can feel truly fulfilled, even without working toward a specific goal.

The same sense of peace can be found in simpler moments, too. Think about spending time with loved ones—whether it's a family gathering, a meal with friends, or simply sitting together silently. In these moments, we are not focused on what needs to be done next or trying to achieve anything. We are simply enjoying the presence of those around us. That's when we feel the most fulfillment—not when striving to impress or accomplish something, but when we allow ourselves to exist in the moment without pressure or expectations.

So why do we feel this peace on vacation or when spending time with loved ones? It's because, in those moments, we give ourselves permission to believe that we have enough. We don't need anything extra to feel complete. But why can't we bring that same mindset into our regular lives? Why can't we experience that same feeling of "enough" on a typical weekend or even in the middle of a busy workday?

The truth is, we already have enough. Enough to be happy, feel fulfilled, and live peacefully with ourselves and the world. When we stop chasing the illusion of 'more'—whether it's more success, more things, or more recognition—we make room for the abundance we already possess. It's not about abandoning our dreams or ambitions but about realizing that contentment doesn't lie in the future; it lives right here, in this moment, in the things we already have. So, take a deep breath, step back, and give yourself permission to be. To recognize that you are enough, just as you are, is one of the most liberating truths you can embrace. And once you do, you'll discover a sense of peace and fulfillment that no goal can match, no matter how big.

CHAPTER 16

YOU ARE NOT ALWAYS IN CONTROL

Humans are social animals, and in our daily interactions with family members, friends, colleagues, and even strangers, we often find ourselves trying to control or influence situations. From small exchanges to major decisions, we instinctively seek control over our environment, relationships, and the outcomes of our actions. But what if we accepted that we won't always be in control? The truth is that embracing this uncertainty can make life so much easier. When we recognize that everyone around us is responding in their own way, doing what they believe is right—just as we are—we begin to understand the need for flexibility. This understanding can prevent us from forming prejudices or jumping to conclusions based on incomplete information.

There will always be someone with a different perspective, just as there will always be someone who rises as a leader in a group—whether due to expertise, influence, or circumstances. Leadership often comes with expectations: the pressure to perform, to maintain authority, and to meet the needs of others. Suppose our goal is to become the leader. In that case, we set ourselves up for a life where personal comfort, likes, and dislikes are often sacrificed to meet those external expectations. We risk becoming driven by forces outside our control, constantly adjusting our actions to fit the mold others expect of us.

On the other hand, if we focus on our well-being first—staying calm, happy, and fulfilled—we can be valuable, contributing members of any group. If leadership comes, it will be because the group chooses us, not because we manipulated our way to the top. This is how true, respected leaders are born. Leadership doesn't start with titles or roles; it begins with us. Suppose we are physically fit, emotionally stable, and willing to help others. In that case, the group we are part of will reflect those qualities, too. After all, we can't offer what we don't possess ourselves.

This principle isn't just applicable to work or formal leadership roles; it extends to every aspect of our lives, including social gatherings and family dynamics. Think about a typical gathering where you're surrounded by friends or relatives. If you're always focused on controlling the outcome—whether it's impressing others, ensuring things go precisely as planned, or orchestrating every conversation—you'll miss the joy of simply being present. Letting go of the need to impress or control frees us to genuinely connect with people. It allows relationships to become more enjoyable and authentic without the constant pressure to manage perceptions or outcomes.

The key here is to focus on self-improvement and recognize that not every situation requires a reaction. Sometimes, the best thing we can do is step back and observe. By accepting that we won't always be in control of what's happening around us, we remove unnecessary stress from our lives. When we release our grip on the need to control everything, we find peace in simply existing and engaging with the world as it comes to us.

At work, we often encounter colleagues with differing skill sets, approaches, and styles of working. It's easy to feel friction when someone doesn't handle things the way we would, but we must coexist with them to ensure the project's success. Instead of viewing this as an obstacle, we can see it as an opportunity to grow. Everyone has their strengths, and we can only control how we contribute to the collective effort. How we conduct ourselves in these situations matters most, as we may be representing our team or company. Still, it ultimately starts with our own actions.

Similarly, think about your hobbies or passions— painting, gardening, or walking in the park. These activities don't demand specific outcomes. We engage in them for the sheer joy of the present moment. They remind us that not everything in life needs a goal; sometimes, the beauty lies in the act itself. Engaging in such activities helps us reconnect with our inner selves. It reminds us that joy can be found in the journey, not just in the destination.

As we move through life, it's easy to get trapped into thinking that happiness lies in the following achievement or milestone. We often tell ourselves, "Once I get that promotion," or "Once I finish this project," happiness will follow. But what if happiness is already around us—in our interactions, moments of stillness, and the things we do purely for joy? We don't always have to earn our contentment. Sometimes, it's simply about allowing ourselves to be present and appreciate what is without needing control or achievement.

Take sports, for example. A player can train as hard as possible for a match, but what the opponent brings to the field is beyond his control. Coaches often base their strategies on the past performance data of the opposing team, assuming their performance would be in tune with their previous games. But this is not always the case. Numerous factors, such as a key player getting sick or injured, can shift the balance of a match. Various uncontrollable variables—weather, luck, travel fatigue, or the players' mood—can influence the outcome. If controlling every aspect of a match were possible, there would never be upsets in sports. But life doesn't work that way. Every athlete knows that time and circumstance change things, and no one stays at the top forever. It's a reminder that control is an illusion, and adapting and accepting what we cannot change is key to moving forward with humility.

Similarly, consider the process of applying for a job. We can ensure we have all the necessary skills and present ourselves as well as possible during the interview. But what other applicants bring to the table is beyond our control. So many factors are at play when landing a job—timing, availability, and even the employer's preferences—go far beyond what's on our resume. When so many forces are involved in even a single job opening, why is it so hard for us to accept that we can't control every outcome around the process of the job hunt? Rejection doesn't always mean we're not qualified; it may mean someone else was in a better position at the right time. Recognizing this allows us to free ourselves from unnecessary stress and pressure.

And yet, many of us put ourselves under immense pressure to achieve career milestones within a set timeframe. We set deadlines for ourselves, telling ourselves we must secure a "better" job by a certain age or a specific moment. This pressure is often self-imposed, born from a belief that we should constantly prove our worth. Understanding why it's time to move on to a better job is a wise decision; however, putting deadlines on things beyond our control is not wise. We must recognize that we can plan for the future but can't force it to happen on our timeline.

So, let's step back and free ourselves from the prison we unknowingly create. By accepting that we won't always be in control of everything around us, we release the constant pressure to manage every detail. This doesn't mean giving up on our goals or desires—it means shifting our focus to what we can control: our mindset, actions, and responses. When we stop fighting against life's natural flow, we allow ourselves to move with it, trusting that things will unfold as they should. Doing so makes room for peace, growth, and genuine fulfillment. Letting go of control is not about abandoning our ambitions; it's about finding freedom in the journey, knowing we are enough just as we are. This is where true freedom begins.

CHAPTER 17

HOW TECHNOLOGY ADDS TO OUR HAPPINESS

Before us, countless civilizations have risen and fallen. Yet today, we stand at the peak of human evolution, with advancements in medicine that continually raise our life expectancy. Once our basic survival needs were met, humanity began to enjoy the many blessings that life today offers. How many of us realize we are the most fortunate generation ever? We have access to countless modes of transportation, instantaneous communication, and a world where regional or national boundaries are becoming increasingly irrelevant. Once a patchwork of isolated nations, the world is now becoming a single, interconnected global village.

Our ability to communicate, travel, and connect with anyone across the globe has made the world feel smaller and more accessible than ever before. Yet, even amid these advancements, we often forget to stop and appreciate the ease with which we live today.

Technology has changed our lives in remarkable ways. With the rapid advancement of science, we now have gadgets and devices designed to make our lives easier.

Consider something as simple as being asked to walk 3 kilometers every day. In the past, we relied on physical markers like maps or landmarks. Now, we don't need to rely on anything external; our smartwatch can tell us exactly how many steps we've taken. In fact, we now live in an era where, without stepping into a diagnostic center, we can monitor our health in real-time—tracking heart rate, blood pressure, and blood sugar levels. In other words, we have created systems that allow us to keep track of almost everything that might require our attention. These advancements make our lives more comfortable and empower us to take charge of our health and well-being. However, despite all these conveniences, keeping track of our emotional and mental health remains untouched by technology.

We can order food with a button, book flights, and manage finances without leaving our homes. At work, we can generate complex reports in seconds, quickly analyzing and adjusting our strategies. But there are things that no gadget can track: how we are feeling, thinking, or processing our experiences and emotions throughout the day. Today, technology can't measure our frame of mind or gauge the undercurrent of stress, joy, or anxiety we carry with us. These internal processes, the very things that influence our decisions, interactions, and reactions, are still something we have to monitor and manage manually. We are ultimately responsible for tuning into ourselves, reflecting on our mental state, and checking in with our emotional well-being.

While we're surrounded by technologies that make our lives easier, it's important to remember that we are the ones in control of how and when we use these tools. Smartphones, laptops, and social media platforms are designed to grab our attention, often pulling us into endless scrolling, liking, and watching cycles. But these gadgets, wonderful as they are, do not have to dictate how we spend our time. Instead, we have the power to decide why we use them.

When we pick up our phone or sit at our computer, let's pause and ask ourself: Why am I using the smartphone now? Or Why am I switching the TV on now? Are we checking in on a social media feed because it's a habit? Or are we purposefully engaging in a conversation, learning something new, or connecting with loved ones?

By clarifying our intention before using these devices, we can prevent ourselves from being pulled into a reactive, autopilot mode where we are constantly driven by external stimuli. This simple act of mindfulness empowers us to remain in control of our lives rather than letting the addictive nature of technology steer us away from the present moment. That said, there is no harm in using these devices for entertainment as long as we know when and how much entertainment is enough. How often does it happen that we end up clicking on a movie or web series trailer while looking for information online? Before we knew it, we spent hours or even days watching that entire series. This is a classic example of technology taking over our attention without us realizing it. It shows how easily we can be pulled into distractions if we're not intentional with how we use our devices.

In a world where technology surrounds us at every turn, it's easy to fall into patterns of mindless use. We unlock our phones out of habit, scroll through feeds without a clear purpose, or reach for our laptops without thinking about whether it's necessary. Take, for example, visiting a new client in their office. It's an unfamiliar space, full of new people, sights, and sounds. While waiting in the reception area, we unknowingly—and often out of habit—reach for our phones. It's our default move, a way to avoid eye contact or appear busy in an unfamiliar environment. There may be no notification to check, but we still don't take our eyes off the screen. This is the habit we've formed, and these moments reveal just how much we've been hijacked by these tools.

But the key to happiness, as we've seen, is recognizing that everything we use—whether it's a device or a relationship, a moment of silence or a social connection—requires attention. Technology is here to make our lives easier, but it should not be used as a default activity. Rather than reaching for your phone out of habit or scrolling aimlessly, ask yourself: What do I need at this moment? Do I need to check a message, search for information, or create something? If the answer is yes, then use the device with purpose. But if the answer is no, step away from the screen and take a moment to reconnect with your surroundings, your body, or your thoughts. It goes without saying that stepping away from the screen is also one of the best things you can do for your eyes, giving them the rest they need from constant exposure to digital devices. In this way, we remain in charge of our actions and are less likely to be overwhelmed by the continuous pull of the digital world.

Technology is a marvel of human ingenuity. Today's devices and apps are incredible creations—designed to simplify our lives, enhance our well-being, and connect us in ways our ancestors could never have imagined. But as powerful as these tools are, it's essential to remember that they should serve us, not the other way around. We live in a time where it's easy to fall into the trap of becoming overly dependent on these technologies. The more we use them without conscious thought, the more we risk losing control over how they influence our lives.

The goal isn't to demonize technology but to recognize that these tools are at their best when we use them deliberately. When we set boundaries and clear intentions, they can add value to our lives. But the moment they begin to dictate our actions or habits, we risk becoming dependent on them. Technology should be our servant, not our master.

While gadgets can tell us how many steps we've taken, they can't tell us how we felt during those steps. How did we react to challenges? How did we handle stress or joy? Understanding our inner world remains a deeply human task.

This is where "me time" comes in. Whether you end your day with reflection or take a few minutes in the morning to collect your thoughts, these moments are essential. It's not that these sessions make us superhuman, but instead, they remind us of our human limitations. These quiet moments help us understand that, no matter how involved we are in the external world, we are still just one small part of a more extensive process. This realization helps us not get carried away by our titles or the power that comes with them.

In these moments of stillness, we confront the reality that we are not the center of the universe, no matter how significant our roles may seem in the grand scheme. This realization fosters humility and a deeper understanding of our place in the world.

Reflecting on ourselves is like taking a shower at the end of the day. Just as we cleanse our bodies of the day's dirt, we also cleanse our minds, letting go of accumulated stress and ego. In those moments of stillness, we begin to see ourselves as minor players in a grand, unfolding drama. We learn to accept things as they are rather than being driven by ego. But of course, that same ego often takes the wheel as soon as we re-enter the outside world.

This is the paradox: the more we realize our smallness in the grand picture, the more our ego works against us, pushing us to take charge and prove ourselves. Our society often encourages us to "go after what we want" and "prove our worth." But in doing so, we may lose touch with our deeper selves.

This is how we've been trained to live in society: we are encouraged to value people who "get things done," constantly moving forward. It becomes nearly impossible to step back and admit our limitations without feeling like we are falling behind. Those addicted to power or fame often live like robots, tirelessly chasing the next goal. The trouble is that robots break down, and so do people. The exhaustion from this constant race is absolute. People give their best until life shows them that not everything is under their control—and that's when they break down.

In a culture that celebrates the relentless pursuit of more, it's easy to believe we must always be on the go. But what happens when we push ourselves past our limits? The truth is that exhaustion, burnout, and mental health struggles don't just happen by accident—they stem from a refusal to acknowledge that we can't control everything.

Refusing to accept reality is often the first step toward mental distress or depression. Learning new things is easy, but unlearning old habits is hard. We're taught to value hard work, embrace competition, and constantly push for more. Some even claim that they are at their best when competing with others. This need for ego validation makes "being better than someone else" more important than simply being good at something.

Competition is ingrained in us from an early age. But we need to ask ourselves: what does it indeed mean to be "better"? Is it about outperforming others or accepting who we are and finding contentment and happiness within our own journey?

If we can step out of this cycle—this constant pursuit of more, this mindset of always wishing for better options— we might begin to see things differently. Look around.

Consider all the machines, devices, and conveniences already at our disposal. How often do we stop being thankful for them? The gadgets we now rely on likely didn't exist a few decades ago. Yet previous generations survived without them. Many people worldwide still have to work harder than we do simply because they don't have access to the same technologies yet. This fact should make us realize that we live in an era of unparalleled luxury.

But we are often trapped in a mindset that devalues what we already have, focusing instead on what we lack. We constantly chase after what we don't have yet while taking everything we already own for granted. Let's pause to reflect on all the innovators, scientists, and visionaries whose inventions have made our lives much more manageable. Their work has shaped the world we live in today—and we often overlook the tremendous gift of that.

By cultivating a mindset of gratitude, we not only recognize the luxury of our time and open ourselves up to a more profound sense of fulfillment. We appreciate what's already here when we stop looking for what's next.

As discussed in the previous chapter, we tend to ignore the beauty around us—whether it's a sunset on the beach or the food on our plates—because we're too distracted by our smartphones. But this habit of ignoring isn't limited to natural beauty; it extends into every area of life. A college student, for example, might be so absorbed in their studies that they miss out on the simple joys of the present. Similarly, professionals can become so fixated on landing the next client, project, or promotion that they forget to appreciate their current achievements.

Please take a moment to think about how we treat the things we own. When we buy a new phone, we treat it with care. We handle it delicately, ensure it's never overcharged or left unattended, and gently place it on the table. But we stop giving it that same attention after a few weeks or months. It is tossed carelessly onto the couch or left charging on the nightstand. The phone itself hasn't changed—it still works the same way—but our attitude toward it has. We take it for granted, and that's where the problem lies. It's not about the phone itself; it's about how we approach the things we own. We stop appreciating them because we've grown accustomed to them.

This mindset extends beyond objects. We often treat relationships, health, and even our own peace of mind the same way. We take them for granted until they start to fade or break down. And only then do we realize how much we've neglected. It's a powerful reminder that everything we own, whether a device or a relationship, deserves our care and attention—not just when it's new or exciting, but always.

As we reflect on the remarkable advancements of our time, it becomes clear that we are living in an era of unprecedented comfort and convenience. We have gadgets tracking our health, technology connecting us across continents, and luxuries our ancestors could never have dreamed of. Yet, in all this abundance, there's one thing we often overlook: the simple, fleeting moments that make up our daily lives. These moments, no matter how small, are where true happiness resides.

Happiness is not something we must chase or achieve. It's already here, in the present moment, waiting for us to recognize it. The technology we use, the luxuries we enjoy, and the opportunities at our fingertips are all incredible gifts. But if we are constantly distracted by what we lack or what we're striving for, we miss out on the one thing that can truly bring us joy: now.

We create space for genuine happiness when we stop chasing the next big thing and start appreciating what we already have. When we step outside the constant rush and pause to reflect, we can see the beauty of our lives as they are without the need for continuous improvement or comparison.

True happiness is not about accumulating more or striving for an idealized future. It is about fully experiencing the present. The comfort of our homes, the food on our tables, the conversations with loved ones—these are all opportunities to feel happiness in its most authentic form. The key is to pause, take a breath, and simply be—to embrace the present as it is, not as we wish it would be.

We have all the tools to live a life filled with meaning and joy. However, the true power lies not in the gadgets we use or the goals we achieve. It lies in our ability to recognize that, amid everything we have, the most valuable thing we can possess is the ability to be happy right now. So, the next time you find yourself distracted or discontent, remember this: the present moment is not something to be rushed through or ignored. It is the only place where true happiness can be found. And it's already here, waiting for you to step into it fully.

CHAPTER 18

TARGETS CAUSE STRESS

There's an old phrase: "God laughs when man makes plans." We've all heard it, but how often do we stop to think about its meaning? From a young age, we're taught that a life without goals or targets is wasted. This idea takes root early, starting with questions like, "What do you want to be when you grow up?" As we age, these questions shift: "How long do you plan to stay at this job?" "When do you expect your next promotion?" "When will you start your own business?" And so on.

It's a never-ending vicious circle. Before we even answer one question, a new one appears. No matter how much we've achieved from birth to the deathbed—whether it's material wealth or wisdom—there always seems to be more to reach out there. We create action plans, set small and big targets, and get trapped in the cycle of achieving them. Ironically, these goals, which we believe will bring us happiness, are often the very things causing us stress. Yet, we don't see this self-inflicted pain because it feels normal to always be planning the next step.

Take, for example, the pressure we put on children. From school assignments to extracurricular activities, we bombard them with goals. They grow up believing that life is about meeting expectations, one after the other. The child who once played freely now schedules time to relax. This constant need to strive for something more ingrains a sense of inadequacy—because no matter how well we do, there's always a new goal waiting around the corner.

Expectations and Disappointments

"Expectation is the first step towards disappointment." We all can live life accepting people and things as they are, but instead, we often choose the path of change. We believe in our ability to improve everything, but time and time again, reality shows us otherwise. Still, our ego refuses to admit we can't control everything. In some situations, we may feel like we're in the driver's seat, but often, we're not. Imagine planning a project involving 20 people with a strict deadline. Logically, 20 potential factors could cause delays— anything from personal emergencies to misunderstandings. And yet, we push forward, making contingency plans and crafting backup strategies. However, like a machine with 100 parts, each part is a potential point of failure. The more complex the system, the more things can go wrong. So why do we keep planning, believing that we alone can dictate outcomes? Understanding that we aren't always in control can help us take a step back. Rather than being emotionally invested in every plan, we can learn to see it for what it is—just a plan, not a promise. This mental shift can relieve us of unnecessary stress.

From Survival to Desire

The urge to set goals doesn't come from nowhere—it starts with a survival instinct. Once our basic needs are met, we begin expanding our ambitions. We aim to help family members, friends, and our community; to do that, we convince ourselves we need more resources. This naturally leads to more desires, more plans, and more deadlines.

But if we start viewing our plans as plans—nothing more, nothing less—they lose their power to define us. We won't be as disappointed if things don't go as expected because we'll understand that outcomes are often beyond our control. It's a simple shift in perspective, but it can change everything. By removing the emotional weight we attach to goals, we create a space for ease.

Real-World Examples

Consider a retiree who has spent their whole life working toward financial security. After retirement, they suddenly find themselves with all the time in the world—but feel lost because they no longer have a goal to chase. This person might take up hobbies not for enjoyment but to fill the void left by a lifetime of planning and achieving. The stress here comes not from a lack of goals but from the inability to relax without them.

Even within a family setting, this cycle continues. Parents may set goals for their children, pushing them to succeed academically, socially, or athletically. The constant planning and striving to create the "perfect" future for their kids often takes away from enjoying the present moment with them. Instead of just appreciating a simple evening together, they're mentally calculating the next steps for their child's success.

For many teenagers, life can feel like an endless checklist. Whether it's doing well in school, excelling in sports, or participating in extracurricular activities, there's a constant expectation to be "building a resume" for the future. Teachers, parents, and peers often ask questions like, "What are your plans after high school?" or "What are you doing to get into a good college?" This creates a sense of pressure to always work toward something more significant.

Imagine a high school student juggling multiple responsibilities—keeping grades up, playing on the soccer team, and joining a few clubs to stand out for college applications. They might constantly think, "I need to get an A on this test," or "I have to make varsity to impress the college scouts." There's this never-ending cycle of setting goals, feeling stress, and worrying about future outcomes.

But what if we hit pause for a moment? What if they allowed themselves to be a teenager instead of constantly chasing the next goal? To enjoy a soccer game for the love of playing, not just because it might lead to a scholarship. To study because learning can be fulfilling, not because it's a means to an end. Or to spend time with friends, not because it's "productive" or boosts their social standing, but because it's fun.

By letting go of the constant pressure to perform and achieve, they could experience life as it happens. Maybe they'd realize more joy playing sports when focusing on the game, not the potential future rewards. Or they might discover that sometimes, the best moments come when you're not working toward any particular goal—like spending a Saturday with friends without worrying about grades or achievements.

A New Way Forward

Think about what you enjoy doing in your spare time - playing an instrument, walking your pets, gardening. These activities don't demand an outcome. You don't play an instrument to get promoted or walk your pets to impress people. You do these things because they make you happy. That's the essence of finding happiness here and now—allowing yourself to do things without attaching an expectation to them.

If we shift this mindset into other areas of life, we might find that the pressure lifts. By letting go of the need to control every outcome and accepting things as they are, we free ourselves from unnecessary stress.

The Balance Between Goals and Presence

The truth is that goals have their place. They drive innovation, help us grow, and structure our lives. But the problem arises when we become consumed by them. When pursuing the next milestone overshadows our ability to enjoy life as it is.

Instead of abandoning ambition, we need to strike a balance. Yes, aim for success and plan for the future, but don't let it rob you of the joy right before you. The key is to approach life's plans flexibly, knowing that things may not always go how we hope. When not rigidly attached to an outcome, we free ourselves from disappointment and open the door to happiness, regardless of what happens next.

Imagine a world where we can work toward our goals without allowing them to define our sense of self-worth. Where success isn't measured by how much we've accumulated or achieved but by how content we feel in the present moment. In this world, goals become guideposts—not prisons.

Letting Life Unfold

Life isn't something we can fully predict or control. The more we try, the more stress and frustration we invite. But when we take a step back and let life unfold, trusting that we'll be okay no matter what, we create space for peace. This isn't about giving up—it's about letting go.

So, the next time you feel pressured to plan, achieve, or meet a deadline, pause and ask yourself: Is this goal bringing me closer to happiness or pulling me further from it? If the answer is the latter, it may be time to reassess.

Because, in the end, happiness doesn't wait for the perfect plan—it's already here in the moments we choose to stop and notice it.

CHAPTER 19

CONNECTING THE DOTS

Recognizing Internal and External Influences

Now that we can see how minute changes in our perspectives towards life can significantly enhance our life experiences, it's vital to recognize the balance between internal and external influences on our emotions. Life gives us many feelings—happiness, excitement, disappointment, anger, and surprise. The key lies in discerning how much of these emotions are self-imposed and how much is influenced by external factors.

For example, consider how you spend your weekends. This is entirely under your control. You can waste it worrying about an upcoming meeting on Monday or fully enjoy the weekend, appreciating it as a well-earned break after a week of hard work. I dreaded Sundays, consumed by thoughts of an upcoming presentation.

Then, I consciously try to savor my Sundays, indulging in activities I love, like hiking and reading. This shift improved my Sundays and made me approach Mondays with a refreshed mind. This fine-tuning of our mindset—understanding what we are doing and why—makes all the difference.

The Importance of 'Me Time'

Daily solitude—often called "meditation" or "me time"—is crucial to cultivating this fine-tuned mindset. This practice helps us monitor our thoughts and gain broader perspectives on life. These moments of self-reflection can expose self-inflicted pains and remind us that we have a choice in how to respond to situations.

Engaging in 'me time' doesn't necessarily mean sitting in a specific posture or being in a particular place to connect with ourselves. It can be as simple as spending a few quiet minutes on your bed each night before falling asleep, a peaceful moment in the morning, or even a few solitary minutes during your commute when there is no noise or music in the background. We observe our mental patterns more frequently during these moments alone with our thoughts. This shift from a micro to a macro perspective allows us to view life with broader, more nuanced insights.

Reflecting on Human Progress

As we gain this broader perspective, we begin to see ourselves within the larger context of humanity. We are just another species on this planet, experiencing the cycle of birth, reproduction, and death. This leads us to ponder profound questions like, "Who am I?", "What is the purpose of this life?", "Who owns this world?" "Who rules it?" and "Why is there poverty in some areas and abundance in others?"

There is nothing inherently right or wrong in this world; all humans are different, and accepting this fact is crucial for moving forward. Wherever the human race has reached today is part of a long journey that involves much effort. As of today, we are the end result of numerous civilizations that lived on this planet before us. Our society today has been shaped by contributions from different corners of the world, and it continues to evolve.

Science and technology have likely accelerated this process. We are not only reaching the moon and other planets to explore what's beyond our planet but also delving into the minute details of the human body. Humanity continues to learn and grow and this process will go on ever after. Given this short life span, let's live it to the fullest before it's over.

It's as if we are all actors on a grand stage, each with a character to play but within a limited time frame. Let's pause and appreciate the grand play we are a part of. Even before we were born, countless people from different generations came up with ideas and innovations that make our lives incredibly easy today. Someone discovered fire, and someone else learned how to harness it.

Someone invented the wheel, and others figured out how to use it for transportation. This is a wonderful world where sharing ideas and advancements has made survival increasingly viable.

Consider what all we have at our service today: electricity, water supply, means of transportation, temperature control, medical facilities, and numerous ways to keep ourselves entertained. We need to acknowledge the abundance around us to cultivate humility.

The best way to express gratitude for everything we are blessed with is by not holding back when contributing to this human race. So, let's respect the life we have been granted and ensure we spread more happiness than we receive.

Personal Practices and Their Benefits

As we adopt this mindset of gratitude and awareness, integrating personal practices like morning reflection becomes more meaningful. I began setting aside ten minutes every morning for quiet contemplation. At first, it felt strange, but gradually, those ten minutes became a sanctuary, a safe space to process my thoughts and feelings, shaping my day positively.

Consider this: What kind of day would you prefer—one filled with frequent smiles or your usual routine? If you choose more smiles, what's stopping you? Often, it's our societal image that holds us back. We fear that smiling without reason makes us appear less serious or sensible.

But what harm does a smile do? A simple smile can brighten someone's day and foster a positive social exchange, creating happiness. Just a smile, without reason, can make your roommate, neighbor, co-worker, family member, or even a stranger on the road feel good without exchanging words.

I recall an experiment I did at work: I chose to greet my colleagues with a warm smile each morning. Initially, it felt forced, but soon, the responses I received were overwhelmingly positive. People seemed more relaxed and cooperative, creating a more pleasant work environment. This small act of smiling helped manifest a more enjoyable and productive workspace. Yes, a smile is a manifestation if we believe in it.

Reflect on your interactions with that short-tempered neighbor or colleague who perpetuates a cycle of negativity. They manifest their miserable world through their actions, often unaware of their intimidating body language that hinders cooperation from others. Conversely, we are accepted more readily when we are not a threat or nuisance. This awareness helps us invest our time and energy mindfully.

Identifying Personal Needs

To further build on this awareness, let's find time for ourselves regularly to examine where we spend our time and energy and why. Identifying what excites one is crucial and unique to each individual. It's okay if you haven't figured it out yet what excites you - awareness is the first step. It's just a matter of getting started to reap the benefits of this habit.

What distinguishes a successful person from an unsuccessful one in the modern world? Is it the ability to plan and execute? No, the most crucial factor is understanding one's own needs. This distinction separates 'a person with a plan' from 'a person without a plan.' Once we truly know what we need, the plans to achieve it naturally take shape. Humanity's most significant challenge today is not knowing what we genuinely need. We are all different; what excites others may not excite us. Similarly, our idea of fun may differ from that of our friends. Therefore, identifying what excites us is a personal journey. We cannot simply copy someone else's passions. It's absolutely okay if we haven't identified our needs yet because, as they say, identifying the problem is half the battle won.

People spend years pursuing hobbies and activities that don't truly excite them simply because they are popular among their friends. It isn't until one takes the time to explore genuine interests that true joy and fulfillment can be found.

Choosing Happiness Intentionally

Enjoying the process of life by observing our reactions to it, we come to understand that while we can't control external factors, we can control our 'me time.' Over time, we develop the ability to see things as they are without biases. Let's choose happiness intentionally and see how quickly it becomes a habit. We won't need to strive to avoid draining situations; we will naturally seek out those filled with smiles and joy.

Let me remind you, this is precisely how we responded to life when we were young. As children, we effortlessly reverted to a 'default happy mode.' Reviving that carefree spirit can significantly improve our lives. Wouldn't it be wonderful to keep the kid in us alive? Smile more, share jokes, and choose laughter over stress or future worries, experiencing firsthand the shift to a happier state. Be the smart one who knows how to go back to the 'default happy mode' soon after being scolded by elders for any mischief. Remember how we used to play, laugh, and move on from minor mishaps? Future worries had a very short shelf life. Our fabulous 'me time' could start anywhere—on the school bus, in the classroom, while riding a bicycle, or even while looking at a book, pretending to be studying. So, let's not shy away from smiling often. Let's not stop ourselves from sharing that joke. Let's purposefully choose a little extra laughter over anything else. Let's experience for ourselves that it's possible to move to a happier zone. The best part? It doesn't cost a penny.

Social Media and Contentment

Have you ever wondered what we seek on social media? We're often looking for joy, information, or simply a distraction. Ask yourself how content you are in your own company, without gadgets. Observing your thoughts can be enlightening. Those who enjoy their own company are not dependent on external factors or gadgets and see the news for what it is without emotional involvement. Conversely, constant social media consumers can be easily misled since based on our digital footprints, there is enough mechanism to monitor and influence our thought pattern.

Think about how we form strong opinions about celebrities or political figures. This often happens without us noticing, influenced by the content we consume. Do you find it easier to make friends with like-minded people and avoid those with differing perspectives or political views? Next time, don't be too harsh on them; like you, they sought distractions but encountered different content. There's a phrase: "Don't blame the messenger," yet even messengers have lost credibility in today's world. Larger media houses often face propaganda allegations, repeatedly exposed yet still sought for distraction. Strange. Engage with your surroundings—people, places, or things—instead of turning to social media. Choose where to invest your time and energy. Social media isn't inherently wrong if you know what you are seeking. Mindless scrolling through reels is a reminder that control over your mind has been surrendered temporarily. But why? Because distractions are continuously sought.

Embracing Change and Living in the Moment

As we mature, part of our journey involves unlearning things. With age and experience, our belief system changes— we drop some things and embrace others to fit into the world. Resistance to change causes friction, often rooted in our inability to accept things as they are. Our belief system updates continually without noticing, surprising us when a situation becomes unacceptable.

My career path once seemed clear-cut, but my interests and experiences evolved, so did my professional aspirations. Initially, this change was difficult to accept, but embracing the new direction ultimately led to greater satisfaction and success. Over time, everything comes under scrutiny—religion, career, personal relationships. Understanding that everything has a shelf life is crucial for navigating emotional rollercoasters. Change is the only constant, and our thoughts are no exception. Reflect on how you've evolved. Opinions, information sources, and abilities to connect dots and read between lines change. Embrace change confidently without being too hard on yourself. Realize that what's meant to make sense will, in its own time. We are all on unique journeys, reacting in our distinctive ways. Realizing that nothing lasts forever can help us fully live in the moment.

When overwhelmed by situations, our first thought is to capture the moment on camera. We frequently see people recording at beaches or hilltops, hoping to revisit those views later. But imagine living the moment instead of clicking it. Life is full of events worth capturing if we are present.

I decided to put my camera away on a recent vacation and fully immerse myself in the experience. The sights, sounds, and interactions felt more prosperous and memorable than any photo could capture. How often do you revisit old-school pictures? That's life: what seems golden now may lose significance over time, not because it wasn't valuable, but because life moves forward.

Next time you feel the urge to capture a moment on your phone or camera, ask yourself if you have fully lived that moment? If yes, then go ahead and capture it and if not then live that moment first. Choose to see and experience life as it is over restricting it to a compressed view on a digital screen. Social media posts may fade, but memories last a lifetime. Prioritize living moments over documenting them. Only you are the actual audience of your life's moments. It's another step towards creating your own experiences rather than trying to impress others with photos. The essence of experiences at a beach, a family gathering, or good times with friends can never be fully captured in words or pictures. So, let's always prioritize living the moment over recording it.

Summary of Key Learnings:

Now, let's summarize some of the key points we've discussed throughout the book:

- **Recognize Internal and External Influences:** Understand the balance between what affects our emotions internally and externally.

- **Engage in 'Me Time':** Spend solitude for self-reflection and mindfulness.

- **Practice Gratitude:** Acknowledge the progress of human civilization and the abundance around us to cultivate humility.

- **Use Genuine Smiles:** Create a positive ripple effect in your social interactions by smiling sincerely.

- **Identify Personal Needs:** Understand what excites and fulfills you rather than following.

- **Prioritize Living in the Moment:** Choose to fully experience life rather than constantly documenting it.

- **Embrace Change:** Accept that life is ever-changing and adapt your beliefs and practices accordingly.

- **Be Mindful of Social Media Usage:** Reflect on how social media affects your contentment and avoid mindless scrolling.

Happiness is not a destination. It's not something we acquire after ticking off a to-do list of achievements, nor is it something that exists only in a perfect future we may never reach. It's already here, woven into the small, fleeting moments we often overlook.

You've now journeyed through different perspectives on happiness—how our thoughts shape our experiences, how external influences affect our emotions, and how simple shifts in awareness can bring profound joy. But the most important realization is this: Happiness is a choice. It is a habit, a way of looking at life, a mindset we can cultivate.

Think of a child who scrapes his knee while playing. He cries for a moment, then soon after, he is back to running with a grin, completely absorbed in the game again. No over-analysis, no dwelling on the pain—just an instinctive return to joy. Somewhere along the way, we lose this ability. But the good news is that we can reclaim it.

What if, instead of endlessly seeking happiness, we simply allowed ourselves to be happy? What if we trained ourselves to see joy in an ordinary morning coffee, in a deep breath of fresh air, in a kind exchange with a stranger?

Life is not waiting to be perfect before it offers happiness. It's happening now. So, smile a little more, laugh a little louder, and don't hold back from embracing the beautiful messiness of it all. The ultimate secret to happiness? Stop searching. It's been with you all along.

All that's left to do now is simple:

Identify Your Happiness !

ACKNOWLEDGEMENTS

The society I was born into continues to shape me in ways I often don't realize, despite the frequent scrutiny it faces. The scientists and innovators who have shaped everything from safety pins to satellites have made my life immeasurably easier—without their contributions, the simplest tasks would have been far more difficult. Above all, I am deeply grateful to the farmers, the quiet stewards of the land whose work sustains my very existence. Their dedication is something I will forever be grateful for. I also want to thank every person I've met along the way. Each of you has contributed, in some way or another, to making this book a reality. Your support, encouragement, and insights have all played a part. And lastly, to Palu the first person who believed these ideas were worth sharing in the form of a book. Your planning and execution were nothing short of remarkable. This book wouldn't have seen the light of day without you. I can't thank you enough.

ABOUT THE AUTHOR
ABHILASH RAJAN

Abhilash Rajan, an astute observer of life and social norms, wrote this book to offer practical perspectives on achieving happiness. With years of thoughtful scrutiny and comparing moral values, he seeks to guide readers towards a simpler, more joyful existence without drastic changes or courses. His insights, derived from paying close attention to life and social behaviors, aim to inspire a lighter, uncomplicated life. He encourages readers to relax and avoid taking life too seriously, trusting that happiness is attainable in the present moment for everyone.